# COUNTRY HOUSE
## *needlepoint*
### FRANCES KENNETT & BELINDA SCARLETT

# COUNTRY HOUSE
# *needlepoint*
## FRANCES KENNETT & BELINDA SCARLETT

CONRAN OCTOPUS

To Louise and Patrick

First published in 1988 by
Conran Octopus Limited
37 Shelton Street
London WC2H 9HN

British Library Cataloguing in Publication Data
Kennett, Frances
    Country house needlepoint.
    1. Canvas embroidery. Designs – Manuals
    I. Title II. Scarlett, Belinda
746.44'2

Editor  Emma Callery
Art Editor  Ruth Prentice
Production  Louise Barratt
Editorial assistant  Simon Willis

ISBN 1 85029 153 5

Printed in Hong Kong by Mandarin Offset

### ACKNOWLEDGMENTS
The authors wish to thank: Jil Shipley for her patience in copying
their work; Petronella Haldane for her help in devising several of
the charts; Clare Everard, Cathy Gayner and Adrienne Johnson
for their generous help with the remaining embroideries, Emma
Callery for the Holly Frame page 45, and Carola Maingot, who
stitched the Belton orange tree cushion, the Sudeley bird, and
assisted with the making up of the projects. The publisher and
authors wish to thank the following for their permission to
photograph the interiors of the houses featured in this book: Lt
Col Cardwell Moore, Administrator, Glamis Castle; B
Bloomfield, Administrator for the National Trust, Uppark; Mr
Oliver, Curator, Wallington; The Duchess of Buccleugh,
Boughton House; J Money, Curator, Leeds Castle; The Lady
Ashcombe, Sudeley Castle; J D Culverhouse, Manager, Burghley
House; Administrator for the National Trust, Standen; D Bowen,
Administrator, Belton House; Mr & Mrs P Palmer, Dorney
Court; B Nodes, Administrator for His Grace the Duke of Atholl,
Blair Castle; Mrs Clutton Brock, Chastleton; The Marquess of
Northampton, Castle Ashby; Dr J Barker, The Brontë Parsonage
Museum; Mrs A Dundas-Bekker, Arniston.

### CREDITS
Charts: Jil Shipley, Photographs: Angelo Hornak (pages 2, 9, 17,
23, 28, 31, 35, 39, 42, 47, 48/9, 52/3, 57, 60/61, 67, 73, 81, 85,
86, 91, 97, 99, 101, 105, 106/7, 111, 117), James Jackson (page
81), Mike Newton (pages 27, 45, 55, 78/9, 100, 118), The Brontë
Society Brontë Parsonage Museum (pages 113, 114), Illustrations:
Robina Green; Technical Illustrations: John Hutchinson;
Embroideries: The Royal School of Needlework (pages 60, 77,
100, 119); Orange Tree: The Chelsea Gardener (page 78/9);
Jewelry: Butler and Wilson (page 100); Royal School of
Needlework for equipment (page 120); Paterna Yarns
(throughout).

# CONTENTS

BLAIR CASTLE  GLAMIS CASTLE

• Dundee

• Edinburgh

Glasgow •

ARNISTON

WALLINGTON • Newcastle-upon-Tyne

BRONTË PARSONAGE

• Liverpool

BELTON HOUSE

BURGHLEY HOUSE

Birmingham • BOUGHTON HOUSE

CASTLE ASHBY

SUDELEY CASTLE

CHASTLETON

Cardiff • 

DORNEY COURT • London

LEEDS CASTLE

UPPARK STANDEN

• Exeter

# INTRODUCTION

Needlepoint has an ancient history. The use of the term 'tapestry work' hints at its beginnings; noble ladies liked to reproduce the effect of expensive, luxurious woven tapestries in their own stitchwork, and indeed, the finest pieces of work date from the 16th century, when the use of tent stitch on a firm, even-woven canvas originated. Generally canvaswork was used for more domestic items, and the finer woven textiles were reserved for grand reception rooms. However, many of the houses visited for this book reveal that the standard of canvaswork was often fine and precious, and the two types of textile were used side by side.

Only the leisured class could afford the time or the money that silks, wools and tent-stitching required, although of the works included here several were made for personal use or as gifts for family and friends, and have a pleasing informality. We have only featured designs which lend themselves to interpretation in slightly coarser mesh than the originals, and where the subject matter lends itself to contemporary settings. Some examples were just too perfect, or too archaic to suggest adaptation.

Looking at the stitchery from the hands of these aristocratic needlewomen puts one in touch with past eras in a unique way. Their observation of the world surrounding them comes alive in intimate, revealing detail. They had turned over strawberry plants, to see how the tendrils joined to the main stem; seen the poppies cut down with the wheat at harvest time; watched the dogs chase the ducks in their estate farmyards, or spied a swan preening among bulrushes. These are personally recalled details, a rich way of connecting with a womanly past not recorded in other histories. Some of the needlepoints were made at momentous times, during imprisonment, or in a period of bereavement, or more happily to celebrate a wedding or a birth.

There are many other houses that could have been included in this book, but space, distance, or other obstacles prevented their use. There are notable collections at Osborne House, Isle of Wight; Parham Park, Sussex; Montacute House, Somerset; Clandon Park, Surrey; Oxburgh Hall, Norfolk; Hardwick Hall, Derbyshire; Canons Ashby House, Northamptonshire; Gawthorpe Hall, Lancashire; Traquair House, Peebles, and Mellerstain and Berwickshire. Less well-known – but interesting for anyone visiting the area – is Muncaster Castle, at Ravenglass in Cumberland, with European as well as English pieces in its collection. Arbury Hall, Warwickshire, is the most beautifully romantic Gothic Revival house, complete in every detail, with stunning embroideries by Elisabeth Twisden. Lastly, we enjoyed a beautiful day in the serenity of Michelham Priory, East Sussex, which houses the small Aileen Jowsey Collection and some samplers, and has a craft exhibition during the summer months. It is not far from Standen, the William Morris house, making a perfect day's outing for anyone interested in decorative arts.

We spent a most enjoyable summer visiting all these beautiful houses, it was an enriching experience, and, we thank all the owners who allowed us to feature their embroideries.

# SEVENTEENTH CENTURY BEDHANGINGS
## Glamis Castle

Glamis Castle is the legendary setting for Shakespeare's tragedy of Macbeth; indeed the sight of its rising towers and turrets makes tales of ambition, royal intrigue and romance abound in the imagination.

Situated a little north of Dundee, it is the hereditary seat of the Earls of Strathmore and Kinghorne, and the family home of Her Majesty Queen Elizabeth, the Queen Mother. The Earls of Strathmore and Kinghorne have lived in Glamis Castle since 1372; a continuity of possession which means that the Castle contains family treasures of extreme rarity and historic value. These include not only the more formal treasures expected in a premier nobleman's house, but also the more personal valuables that remain preserved only with great care and close attention to detail.

A fascinating note in family records reminds us that the skill of embroidery was esteemed so highly in the 16th and 17th centuries that a craftswoman is mentioned as the prerequisite of the lady of the house. The 8th Lord Glamis, Chancellor of Scotland and Keeper of the Great Seal, was noted for the richness yet sober good order of his household. He kept a principal 'servitor and maister stabular, 2 servitors, a musicianer, master cook and browster [for the bakehouse and brewhouse respectively], foremen, a maister porter and his servant, a grieve [farm bailiff] and an officer'. His lady employed '2 gentlewomen, a browdinstar [embroiderer], a lotrix [bedmaker] and two other female servants'. Family treasures include a jester's motley suit that belonged to the 'private buffoon' employed by Patrick, the 3rd Earl of Kinghorne in the 1680s – the very last nobleman in Scotland to do so.

There are rare and beautiful tapestries dating from the 17th century with scenes from the life of King Nebuchadnezzar – the only others similar are in Knole Castle, Kent, and Powys Castle, in Wales. A pair of needlework panels of the same period depict the sacrifice of Isaac and the return of Jacob. These were made by ladies of the house and show the gentlemen wearing dashing cavalier hats and fashionably luxurious whiskers.

The pieces chosen for this collection were worked by the wife of the 3rd Earl, who kept the jester. Lady Helen Middleton originally made them for bedhangings for a four-poster and they are dated 1683. Now they are used as wallhangings in a room commemorating King Malcolm II who died in 1034, most probably in a hunting lodge built on the site before the Castle.

Most remarkable in these hangings is the wonderful use of embroidery and appliqué in combination. The needlepoint motifs were originally worked close together in tent stitch, on a suitable canvas-type fabric. They were then cut out and attached onto a rich background textile, in this instance a blue linen. Such embroideries are known as 'slips'. To soften the edges, a couched thread is stitched over in sympathetic colourings. Quite freely worked star and dot embroidery is added around the motifs, giving a sparkling richness that has not been lost, even after hundreds of years. The illustration also reveals naïve little birds and animals such as seagulls and deer, embroidered onto the hangings between the more formal symbolic designs, the whole effect being one of great freshness as well as grandeur.

A greedy seagull, one of the lively, naturalistic bird and animal embroideries which are appliquéd on to the blue linen of Glamis, originally made as bedhangings.

The bedhangings at Glamis, covered in 'slips'. The word indicates the origin of the embroidered motifs, being cuttings (or slips) taken from favoured garden plants and used in the designs.

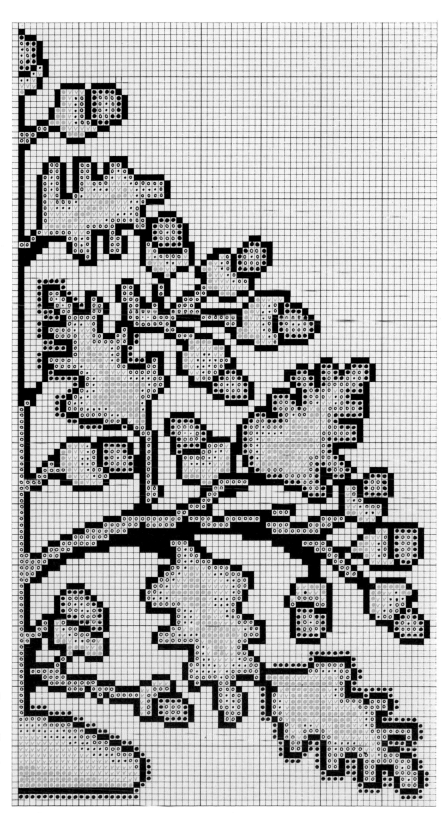

centre

*Left: This 'slip' from the hangings at Glamis shows the sparkling quality that the embroidery round the appliqué work adds to the needlepoint. Intricate flowers are combined with naïve animals to give a lively, endlessly interesting surface decoration to the linen cloth.*

**Oak Tree**

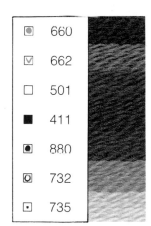

| | |
|---|---|
| ◉ | 660 |
| ☑ | 662 |
| ☐ | 501 |
| ■ | 411 |
| ◙ | 880 |
| ⊡ | 732 |
| · | 735 |

**Calculating Yarn Amounts:** See page 121.
**Canvas requirements:** To make a 36cm/14in square cushion you will need 50cms/20ins square of 10 holes to the inch mesh.

11

centre

**Thistle** (LEFT)

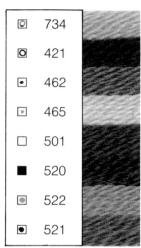

| | |
|---|---|
| ⊡ | 734 |
| ◉ | 421 |
| ⊡ | 462 |
| ▦ | 465 |
| ☐ | 501 |
| ■ | 520 |
| ◉ | 522 |
| ◑ | 521 |

**Calculating Yarn Amounts:**
See page 121.
**Canvas requirements:** To
make a 38cm/15in square
cushion you will need
53cms/21ins square of 10
holes to the inch mesh.

**Border** (RIGHT)

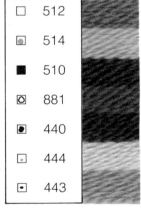

| | |
|---|---|
| ☐ | 512 |
| ◩ | 514 |
| ■ | 510 |
| ◉ | 881 |
| ◑ | 440 |
| ⊡ | 444 |
| ⊡ | 443 |

**Calculating Yarn Amounts:**
See page 121.
**Canvas requirements:** To
make a belt 91cms/36ins by
7.5cms/3ins you will need
107cms/42ins by 23cms/9ins
of 10 holes to the inch mesh.

*Right: The thistle motif
from the hangings at
Glamis Castle lends
itself to many different
colourings. Vivid greens
and purples, or softer
sage and lavender make
it adaptable. Grays,
whites and touches of
yellow against a blue
background suggest a
different mood. The
flower itself is small and
if used for a cushion the
area could be increased
by adding a border –
look at the simple one
on the Belton cushions,
page 74.*

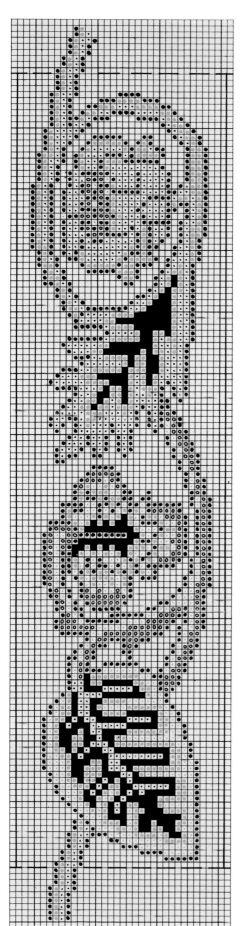

*This delightful hazelnut border has a vivid realism typical of the work on the slips at Glamis. The nuts are ripe for hoarding, and suggested its use for a store of trinkets or useful small objects. The colouring suggested here emulates the faded tones left to us now from the original, but the border would look striking in other rich russet tones with gold accents.*

14

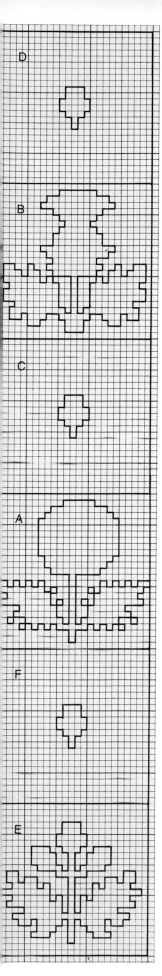

### Oak, Thistle and Rose

| | |
|---|---|
| ◉ | 430 |
| ☑ | 740 |
| ⊡ | 702 |
| ☒ | 200 |
| ⊞ | 903 |
| ◨ | 492 |
| ◉ | 662 |
| ☑ | 663 |
| ☑ | 602 |
| ⊡ | 204 |
| ⊞ | 744 |
| ◉ | 693 |
| A | 503 |
| B | 490 |
| C | 871 |
| D | 741 |
| E | 912 |
| F | 433 |

**Calculating Yarn Amounts:**
See page 121.
**Canvas requirements:** To make a 38cm/15in square cushion you will need 53cms/21ins square of 5 holes to the inch mesh.

*The elements from the Glamis hangings are simplified here to inspire various schemes for combining them. You could just as easily use only one or two elements, and play with the colours between thistles and roses, or just big and little acorns too. And of course the beauty of this plan is that cushion covers, folder covers, even small boxes, can be made by building up the squares to suitable dimensions.*

# A DAIRY MAID'S FOOT STOOL

## Uppark

Uppark commands a wonderful view over the South Downs, and in its turn creates a splendid vista, its rich red brickwork set off by elaborate stone dressings on the façade. It was built in 1690, but it came into its own when Matthew Fetherstonhaugh inherited a fortune, acquired a baronetcy and a wife, Sarah Lethieullier, and set about filling the interior with a priceless collection of decorations. The house now stands as a magnificent display of Regency taste, with its fine furnishings, Italian rococo plasterwork and European paintings.

Their only son, Sir Harry, continued the family tradition by enlarging the house and entertaining lavishly. One of his frequent guests was the Prince Regent, who used to enjoy horse-racing on the Downs, and the young Emma Hart (later Emma Hamilton) once danced on the dining table for a lark. In later life, though, Sir Harry declined in spirits and became reclusive, until, in 1825, he fell in love with his head dairy maid, Mary Anne Bullock.

The dairy is in the tradition of Marie Antoinette, who used to like dressing up as a shepherdess at Versailles, and would scamper after the sheep in her ornamental gardens. When she became tired, the servants would lay out a picnic on the lawns for her and her entourage. Sir Harry, too, liked to turn his hand to domestic activities, and at Uppark had a 'mock dairy' arranged where he and his fellow guests from London could turn the butter churn for a while and indulge their whim for the rustic life.

Sir Harry sent Mary Anne to Paris for an education, and married her when she was twenty years of age and he was seventy. The couple lived together happily until Sir Harry's death at the age of ninety-two, and his widow continued to care for the house meticulously. On her death in 1874, her sister, Frances, who had also been educated by Sir Harry, succeeded to the estate and assumed the family name of Fetherstonhaugh. She lived on at Uppark until 1895 with her former governess, a Miss Sutherland, for company (rumour suggested she was in fact the natural daughter of Sir Harry).

H. G. Wells' mother was housekeeper at Uppark for thirteen years, when Frances and her companion were old ladies. During a particularly bleak winter, when the inhabitants were snowbound, he produced a newspaper, *The Uppark Alarmist*, and staged little plays for the servants. He described how 'The place had a great effect on me; it retained a vitality that altogether overshadowed the insignificant ebbing trickle of upstairs life, the two elderly ladies in the parlour following their shrunken routines. . .'

That gaiety is apparent in many of the details in the house. Lady Mary Anne was a tireless embroiderer in her widowhood, and made the little footstool that is included here. It is quite simple, and has a fresh, pretty colouring. Much of the furniture retains its earlier 18th-century and early 19th-century coverings. The tapestries and textiles at Uppark are one of the house's great treasures, many pieces finely restored in the 1930s by Lady Meade-Fetherstonhaugh. She discovered that a plant in the garden, 'Bouncing Bet' (*Saponaria officinalis*), produces a soap-like foam in water which is perfect for restoring old textiles without harming them, and it is used by other conservationists to this day.

The 19th-century design looks unusually fresh, needing no reworking to fit into a modern interior. Only the canvas mesh has been changed for easier stitching.

This pretty flower basket was embroidered for a footstool by a dairy maid at Uppark. She later became mistress of the house on her marriage to Sir Harry Fetherstonhaugh.

centre

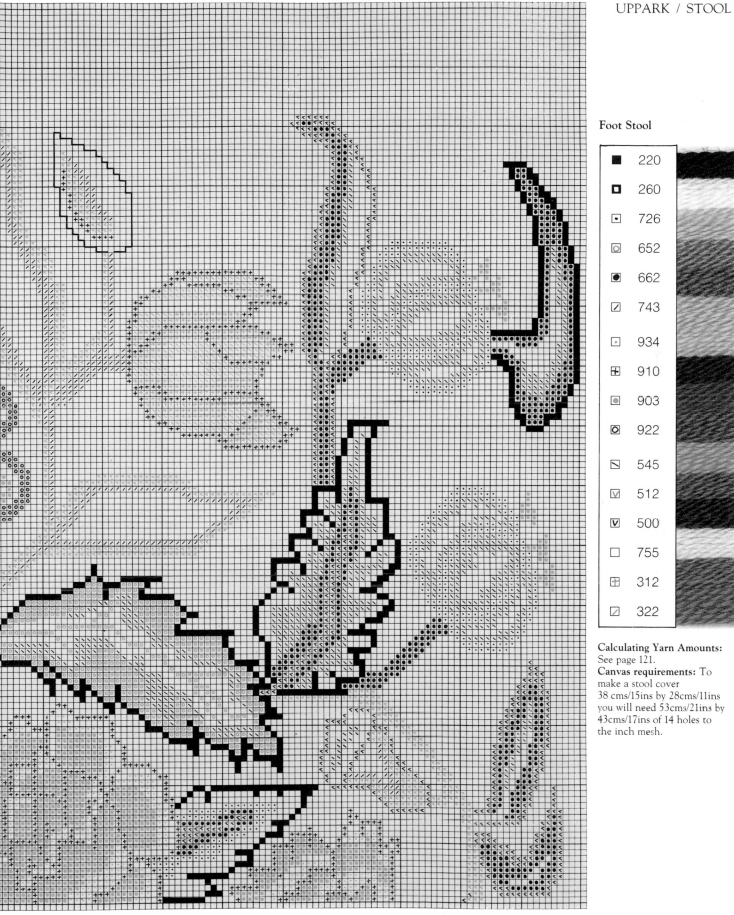

**Foot Stool**

| | |
|---|---|
| ■ | 220 |
| ▫ | 260 |
| ⊡ | 726 |
| ◪ | 652 |
| ◉ | 662 |
| ☑ | 743 |
| ⊡ | 934 |
| ⊞ | 910 |
| ◉ | 903 |
| ◎ | 922 |
| ◩ | 545 |
| ☑ | 512 |
| ☑ | 500 |
| ☐ | 755 |
| ⊞ | 312 |
| ☑ | 322 |

**Calculating Yarn Amounts:** See page 121.
**Canvas requirements:** To make a stool cover 38 cms/15ins by 28cms/11ins you will need 53cms/21ins by 43cms/17ins of 14 holes to the inch mesh.

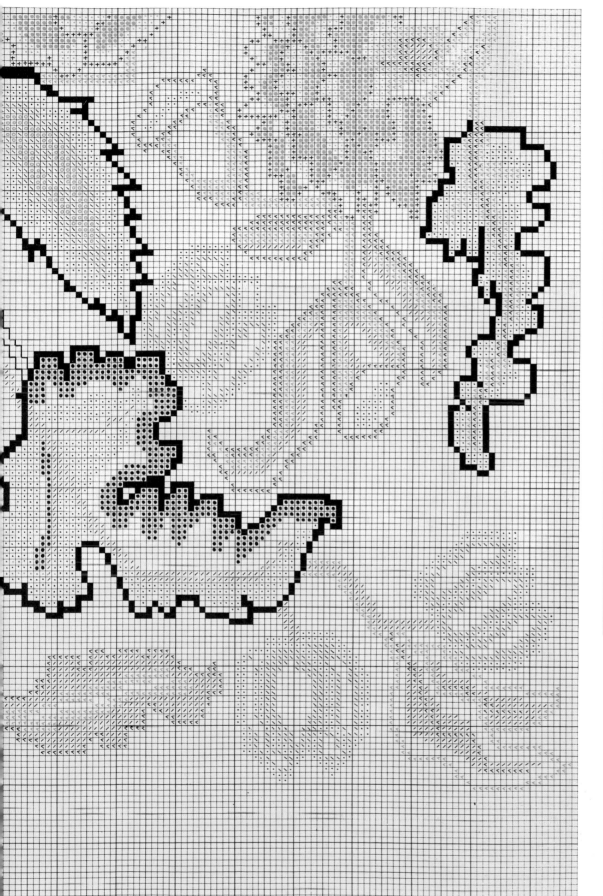

**Foot Stool**

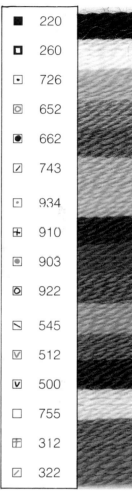

| Symbol | Code |
|--------|------|
| ■ | 220 |
| ▢ | 260 |
| ⊡ | 726 |
| ◎ | 652 |
| ◉ | 662 |
| ◪ | 743 |
| ⊡ | 934 |
| ⊞ | 910 |
| ◉ | 903 |
| ◎ | 922 |
| ◩ | 545 |
| ☑ | 512 |
| ☑ | 500 |
| ▢ | 755 |
| ⊞ | 312 |
| ◪ | 322 |

**Calculating Yarn Amounts:**
See page 121.
**Canvas requirements:** To
make a stool cover
38 cms/15ins by 28cms/11ins
you will need 53cms/21ins by
43cms/17ins of 14 holes to
the inch mesh.

# A Nursery Sampler and Folding Screen

## Wallington

Wallington lies in the Middle Marches of Northumberland, favoured with poetic descriptions in the Border Ballads. Not far is Battle Hill, the site of Chevy Chase, where Hotspur and Douglas fought and Douglas lost his life – the subject of one of the oldest poems. Wallington is only twenty miles from Hadrian's Wall and the warlike border family, the Fenwicks, once held it as a moorland castle.

The present square building springs from someone no less belligerent, though in trade, not warfare. Sir Walter Blackett was an eminent Newcastle merchant and an owner of coal and lead mines, and it was he who commissioned the building. His nephew Walter Calverley inherited from him, and, a man of great taste and intelligence, he transformed the interior, exterior and gardens into magnificence.

This same man's mother, Julia Blackett, was a great needlewoman. Ten panels of her work are used as wall-hangings, and are dated 1717. They show exotic Indian-style climbing plants of the kind more often seen in crewel work. A folding screen containing six more panels was placed in the house after her death in 1727. The screen, with designs partly based on engravings by Hollar in a 1653 edition of Virgil's *Eclogues* and *Georgics*, is one of the most valuable objects in the house. Other sources were also used such as engravings by Francis Cleyn, artistic director of the Mortlake tapestry factory, which are directly copied in the stitchery. Motifs are often used without relation to each other in scale, and with a highly imaginative background of exotic trees and mythical birds. Her husband's diary relates that the last panel was completed on 27 February 1716, and that the work in tent stitch took three and a half years, with the help of assistants.

Sir Walter Calverley having no heirs, Wallington passed through his sister's son into an ancient Cornish family, the Trevelyans. The house came into its own as the scene of many gatherings of the flower of 18th- and 19th-century intellectual life: Sir John, the 5th Baronet, like his father before him, was a man of letters and science, and one of the first members of the Royal Horticultural Society. His wife, Maria, was so deeply attached to Wallington that she remained living there after her husband returned to their other family seat, Nettlecombe, in Somerset.

The Trevelyans inclined to benevolent patronage, social organization, radical politics and academic study. Pauline, wife of Sir Walter Calverley Trevelyan, was a botanist, and a close friend of Ruskin, Swinburne, Millais, and Christina Rossetti. Several members of the Pre-Raphaelite Brotherhood and their friends stayed at Wallington. Pauline also provides a link with the talent for handwork, already a tradition in the family. She was a patron of the lace-makers of Devon, and produced many Pre-Raphaelite designs for them.

Altogether, Wallington is not only a treasury of history, but a vivid record of generations of a distinguished family's interests and achievements. Space only allows for two details from the screen made by Julia Blackett. They show considerable skill, are finely observed and sensitively coloured, typifying the qualities of the owners of Wallington: artistic, serious-minded, and diligent.

A strawberry plant from the Wallington screen shows how accurate and vital the embroidery is; any detail from this panel inspires needlepoint ideas.

The sampler from Wallington hangs in the nursery, surrounded by original toys. Try substituting your own house outline for a unique family heirloom.

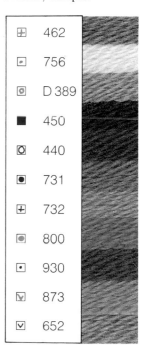

**Nursery Sampler**

| | |
|---|---|
| ⊞ | 462 |
| ⊡ | 756 |
| ◉ | D 389 |
| ■ | 450 |
| ◎ | 440 |
| ◉ | 731 |
| ⊞ | 732 |
| ◉ | 800 |
| ⊡ | 930 |
| ⊻ | 873 |
| ⊻ | 652 |

**Calculating Yarn Amounts:**
See page 121.
**Canvas requirements:** To
make this sampler you will
need 63cms/25ins by
61cms/24ins of 10 holes to
the inch mesh.

## Nursery Rug

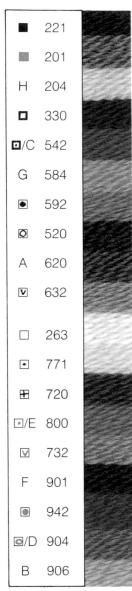

| | |
|---|---|
| ■ | 221 |
| ▧ | 201 |
| H | 204 |
| ▢ | 330 |
| ▣/C | 542 |
| G | 584 |
| ◉ | 592 |
| ◎ | 520 |
| A | 620 |
| ☑ | 632 |
| □ | 263 |
| ⊡ | 771 |
| ⊞ | 720 |
| ▣/E | 800 |
| ☑ | 732 |
| F | 901 |
| ◉ | 942 |
| ◩/D | 904 |
| B | 906 |

**Calculating Yarn Amounts:** See page 121.
**Canvas requirements:** To make this rug you will need 96cms/38ins by 76cms/30ins of 5 holes to the inch mesh. The scale is enlarged by working on 5 mesh rug canvas. If this is difficult to find, you can easily work on 10 mesh canvas, going over two holes for every stitch.

26

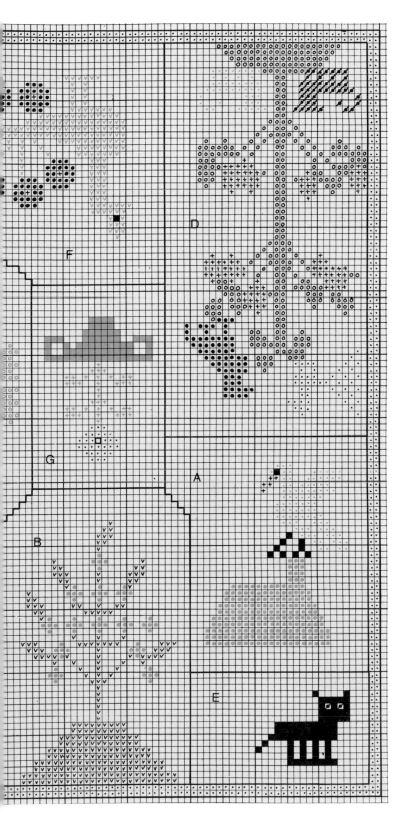

*This lively design for a
nursery rug is based on the
various elements in the
Wallington sampler.
Cross stitch was used –
continental tent stitch
method in one direction and
half cross on the return row
for economy of yarn.*

A section from the
Wallington screen, which is
one of the rarest objects of
the house, typifies the lively
realism of the embroidery.
Observed natural detail is
blended with mythical and
classical figures. Two small
areas have been charted
from this panel, the swan
and the strawberry.

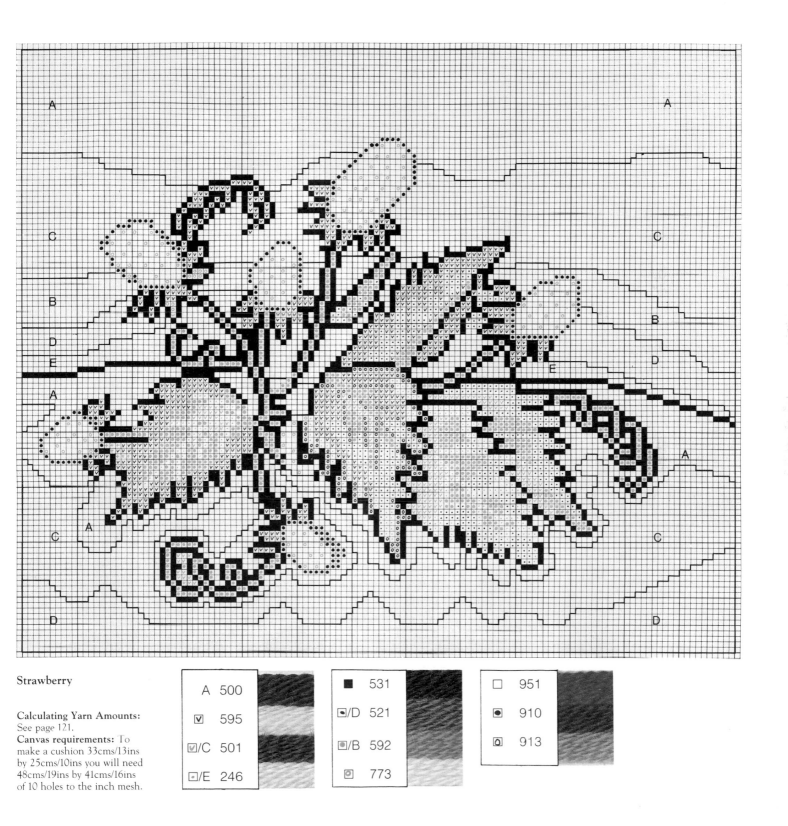

## Strawberry

**Calculating Yarn Amounts:**
See page 121.
**Canvas requirements:** To
make a cushion 33cms/13ins
by 25cms/10ins you will need
48cms/19ins by 41cms/16ins
of 10 holes to the inch mesh.

| | | |
|---|---|---|
| A | 500 | |
| ☑ | 595 | |
| ☑/C | 501 | |
| ☑/E | 246 | |

| | | |
|---|---|---|
| ■ | 531 | |
| ☑/D | 521 | |
| ☑/B | 592 | |
| ☑ | 773 | |

| | | |
|---|---|---|
| ☐ | 951 | |
| ☑ | 910 | |
| ☑ | 913 | |

## Swan

**Calculating Yarn Amounts:**
See page 121.
**Canvas requirements:** To
make a cushion 33cms/13ins
by 28cms/11ins you will need
48cms/19ins by 43cms/17ins
of 10 holes to the inch mesh.

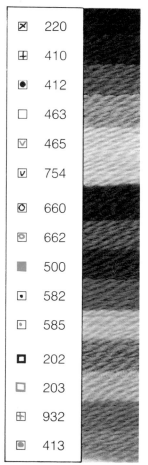

| | |
|---|---|
| ⊠ | 220 |
| ⊞ | 410 |
| ⦿ | 412 |
| ☐ | 463 |
| ☑ | 465 |
| ☑ | 754 |
| ◎ | 660 |
| ◙ | 662 |
| ◼ | 500 |
| ⊡ | 582 |
| ⊡ | 585 |
| ◼ | 202 |
| ☐ | 203 |
| ⊞ | 932 |
| ◙ | 413 |

### Floral Wreath

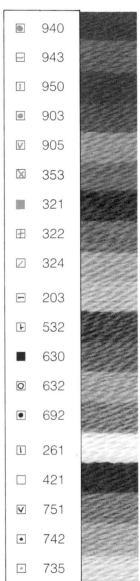

| | |
|---|---|
| ◉ | 940 |
| ⊟ | 943 |
| 🔟 | 950 |
| ◉ | 903 |
| ☑ | 905 |
| ☒ | 353 |
| ◼ | 321 |
| ⊞ | 322 |
| ☑ | 324 |
| ⊟ | 203 |
| ⊩ | 532 |
| ■ | 630 |
| ◎ | 632 |
| ◉ | 692 |
| 🔟 | 261 |
| ☐ | 421 |
| ☑ | 751 |
| ◉ | 742 |
| ◙ | 735 |

**Calculating Yarn Amounts:**
See page 121.
**Canvas requirements:** To
make a frame or mat of
23cms/9ins diameter you will
need 38cms/15ins diameter of
10 holes to the inch mesh.
*The panelled border of the
Wallington Screen inspired
this pretty floral wreath
chart (right). Adjustments
to the design harmonize the
flower motifs with the
circular frame.*

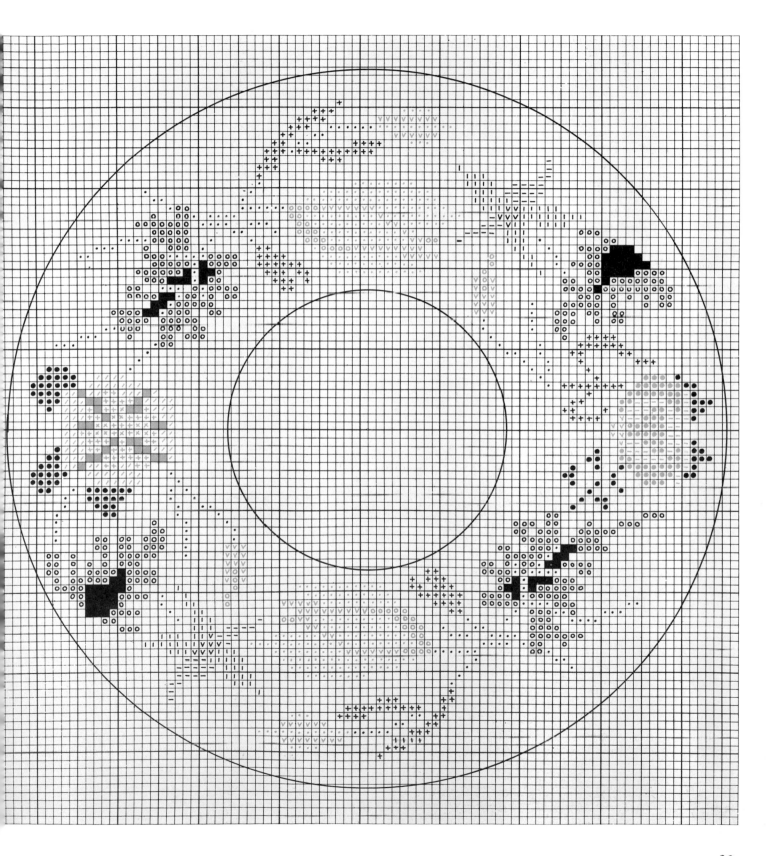

# VICTORIAN CUSHIONS
## Boughton House

Boughton is set in the wide, curving, low hills of Northamptonshire. Long vistas lead the eye to the imposing classical French frontage and mansard roofing of the house – it is nothing less than a French chateau.

A monastery stood on the site when Sir Edward Montagu, Lord Chief Justice to Henry VIII, bought the land and added a manor house to the Great Hall of the monks. Later generations added more wings and courts until the final stage of its development – the building of the north front in the 1690s, created by Ralph, 1st Duke of Montagu, who had been ambassador in Paris and loved all things French. So, in reality, the imposing European exterior covers a collection of buildings with a tradition that is particularly English.

The Duke spent five more years in exile in France for his support of the Duke of Monmouth's rebellion against James II, but returned to favour when King William and Queen Mary came to the throne in 1689. He was created Earl by the King, and then Duke in 1705 by Queen Anne. He was a great patron of the arts, amassing a distinguished and valuable collection of paintings and furniture. He also bought the famous Mortlake tapestry factory in London and ran it for seventeen years, between 1674 and 1691 – fine examples made by the factory adorn the house, including several sets of tapestries and some table covers incorporating the Duke's coat of arms.

A later descendant, the Marquis of Monthermer, lived only long enough to make the Grand Tour of Italy and France, adding yet more beautiful items to the interior of Boughton. On his death, his sister Elizabeth inherited the house and combined the family name with that of her husband, the Duke of Buccleuch, to form Montagu Douglas Scott. Boughton has remained the home of the Dukes of Buccleuch and Queensbury ever since, maintaining a direct family link of over 450 years.

The priceless works of art at Boughton include paintings by El Greco, Teniers, Monnoyer, Van Dyck, to mention only a few, but for all its grandeur the house has a warm atmosphere. The furnishings are harmonious and in no sense suggest the impersonality of a museum. Numerous tapestries and embroideries add to the impression, while ranging in quality and importance from the sublime to the purely domestic.

In the first category is a set of hangings originally made in the 17th century for a state bed in Hungarian point using a cream silk ground with wool floral sprays of red, blue and brown. The colour scheme is still jewel-like in its intensity, though obviously in its day the effect was yet more brilliant.

The two chosen cushions, on the other hand, are just delightful domestic pieces, of a strongly nostalgic, late Victorian style. They were made by Louisa Jane, Countess of Dalkeith (accounting for the crossed 'L'), who was the wife of the 6th Duke of Buccleuch. The cat cushion is matched by a tiny cushion with a coronet on it, obviously done by the same hand, and suggesting that these were made early in her life before her husband succeeded to the dukedom. The present Duchess of Buccleuch takes great interest in the embroideries of Boughton, and actively promotes the craft of embroidery by supporting the Royal School of Needlework in London.

The Royal School of Needlework owns a canvas of a dog on a cushion, similar to that at Boughton. No doubt aristocratic owners liked this affectionate pose.

The noble cat and the Countess of Dalkeith's monogrammed rose wreath have a Victorian charm that is worth reviving. Other palettes could work just as well.

34

*Left: The Boughton rose wreath in its original form is embroidered in unusual autumnal tones, perhaps to suit individual preference, or its original setting. The temptation to rework it in light summery colours is irresistible; fresh yellows, bright pinks, and apple-green shades have been suggested as an alternative.*

**Calculating Yarn Amounts:** See page 121.

**Canvas requirements:** To make a 30cm/12in square cushion you will need 46cms/18ins square of 10 holes to the inch mesh.

### Rosebud Circlet Alternative colourway

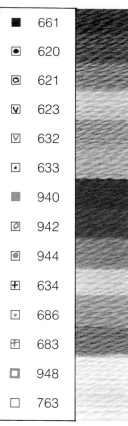

| | |
|---|---|
| ■ | 661 |
| ◉ | 620 |
| ◎ | 621 |
| ⋁ | 623 |
| ⋁ | 632 |
| ⋅ | 633 |
| ▨ | 940 |
| ◪ | 942 |
| ◉ | 944 |
| ⊞ | 634 |
| ⊡ | 686 |
| ⊞ | 683 |
| ▫ | 948 |
| ▫ | 763 |

### Original colourway

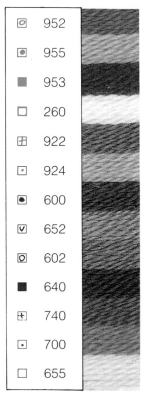

| | |
|---|---|
| ◪ | 952 |
| ◉ | 955 |
| ▨ | 953 |
| ▫ | 260 |
| ⊞ | 922 |
| ⊡ | 924 |
| ◉ | 600 |
| ⋁ | 652 |
| ◎ | 602 |
| ■ | 640 |
| ⊞ | 740 |
| ⋅ | 700 |
| ▫ | 655 |

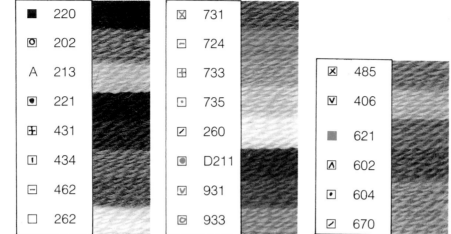

| | | | | | | |
|---|---|---|---|---|---|---|
| ■ | 220 | ⊠ | 731 | ⊠ | 485 |
| ◉ | 202 | ⊟ | 724 | ☑ | 406 |
| A | 213 | ⊞ | 733 | ▪ | 621 |
| ◉ | 221 | ⊡ | 735 | ◭ | 602 |
| ⊞ | 431 | ☑ | 260 | ⊡ | 604 |
| ⊺ | 434 | ◉ | D211 | ☑ | 670 |
| ⊟ | 462 | ☑ | 931 | | |
| ☐ | 262 | ◖ | 933 | | |

**Cat on Cushion**
**Calculating Yarn Amounts:**
See page 121.
**Canvas requirements:** To
make a cushion 30cms/12ins
by 23cms/9ins you will need
46cms/18ins by 38cms/15ins
of 10 holes to the inch mesh.

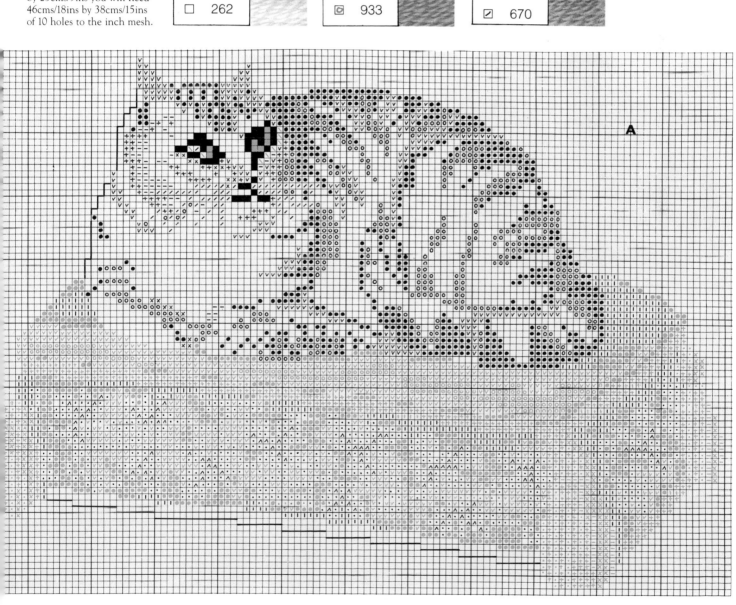

# AN ENGLISH CHAIR AND FLEMISH TAPESTRY

## Leeds Castle

Leeds Castle was built of stone by a Norman Baron in the reign of William the Conqueror's son, Henry I, 900 years ago. It is justly famous as the most romantic of all English castles, having been raised on an island, surrounded by a moat, on the site of a Kentish thane's stronghold. It became royal property on the accession of Edward I, and for 300 years thereafter was a royal palace and, more particularly, a 'lady's castle', for it was the home of six medieval queens; one of its first occupants was the Spanish princess, Eleanor of Castile, the 'chère reine' commemorated with the 'Charing' Cross in London.

Henry VIII enjoyed hunting at Leeds and brought his wife Anne Boleyn to live there. He turned a fortress into a magnificent palace, adding a banqueting hall among other improvements and enlargements. Henry was responsible for the Castle moving out of royal ownership, granting it to Sir Anthony St Leger for services to the crown. One of his descendants financed Sir Walter Raleigh's expedition to search for 'Eldorado'; losing a fortune on its failure, he had to sell Leeds to a relative, Sir Richard Smith.

Various other notable English families owned the Castle in recent history: the Culpepers and the Fairfaxes (both of whom figure largely in American colonial history), and finally Lady Baillie, daughter of Lord Queensborough. She was responsible for the restoration of the Castle and its gardens, and ultimately brought over Stéphane Boudin, the internationally known decorator, and his work at the Castle remains intact today. Under Lady Baillie's aegis, Leeds Castle became a social centre for the *beau monde* of the thirties: Edward VIII, when Prince of Wales, and Prince George, Duke of Kent, were frequent visitors, as were many famous politicians and diplomats.

Lady Baillie was linked through her American mother's family, the Whitneys, to Henry VIII and it seems fitting that she should be the last owner of the Castle and the one who left it to the nation in perpetuity. Its past role was as a lady's castle, and a great lady was appropriately its last owner.

There are many valuable objects in the Castle – paintings, furniture, armoury – besides the value of the structure itself. An impressive reconstruction of rooms for the Queen of Henry V, Catherine de Valois, is complete with 15th-century day-bed, removable for the Queen's progress from palace to palace, and a silk damask woven in France specifically for Leeds with the 'H' and 'C' of the royal couple tied in a lover's knot. The Castle houses several fine Brussels tapestries, and in the banqueting hall, a Flemish tapestry woven around 1500 portraying the Adoration of the Magi, has been chosen for the border designs shown here. The Thorpe Hall room contains very fine 18th-century furniture, including an embroidered firescreen, and a curious card table with a *petit-point* design depicting a flower basket at its centre and playing cards and loose change scattered on its surface. Our other design is taken from a Charles I oak armchair possibly re-covered at a later date. It sits in John Money's office, the administrator who worked closely with Lady Baillie and continues to run Leeds to her standards. A workroom nearby occupies two seamstress-embroiderers who do careful conservation work on the bedhangings, chair covers, and wall-hangings.

A curious central twist taken from the holly design has been simplified for a mirror-image needlepoint chart. Single leaves could be used for smaller projects.

This holly-embroidered oak chair at Leeds dates from the age of Charles I, one of many valuable items collected by Lady Baillie who restored the Castle magnificently.

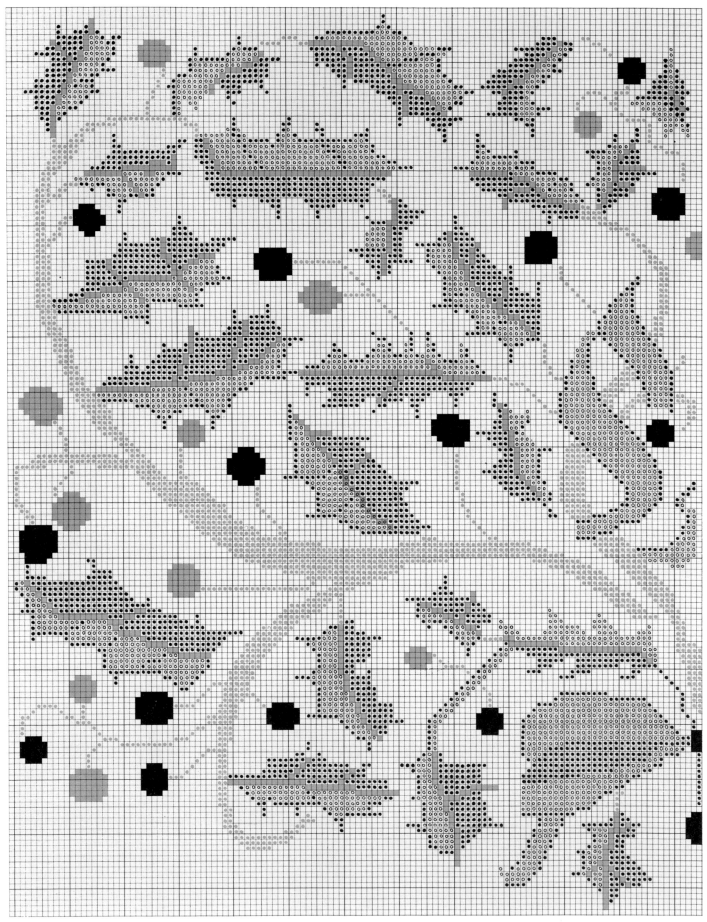

centre

**Holly Chair** (left)

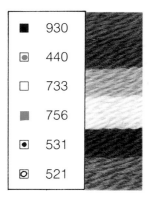

| | |
|---|---|
| ■ | 930 |
| ◉ | 440 |
| □ | 733 |
| ▦ | 756 |
| ◉ | 531 |
| ◎ | 521 |

**Calculating Yarn Amounts:**
See page 121.
**Canvas requirements:** To
make a chair seat cover or
bolster cushion of
63cms/25ins by 43cms/17ins
you will need 79cms/31ins by
58cms/23ins of 10 holes to
the inch mesh.

**Holly Frame** (Right)

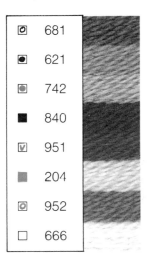

| | |
|---|---|
| ◎ | 681 |
| ◉ | 621 |
| ◉ | 742 |
| ■ | 840 |
| ☑ | 951 |
| ▦ | 204 |
| ◎ | 952 |
| □ | 666 |

**Calculating Yarn Amounts:**
See page 121.
**Canvas requirements:** To
make this frame you will
need 41cms/16ins by
36cms/14ins of 10 holes to
the inch mesh. The centre
can be filled in to suit the
dimensions of your mirror or
picture.

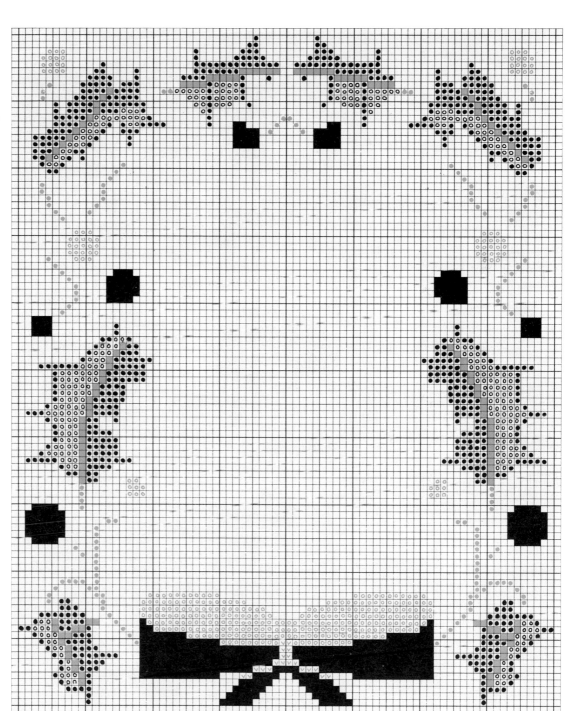

## Wave Border

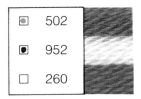

| ◉ | 502 |
| ◉ | 952 |
| □ | 260 |

**Calculating Yarn Amounts:**
See page 121.
**Canvas requirements:** To
make this frame you will
need 36cms/14ins square of
10 holes to the inch mesh.
The centre square can be
filled in to suit the
dimensions of your mirror or
picture.

*Left: Tapestries can yield
very beautiful pattern ideas
for embroidery. Both the
twisted ribbon and the wave
pattern borders from this
beautiful Brussels tapestry
hanging at Leeds Castle
have been adapted as
frame, belt, or tie-back
projects in needlepoint. The
balanced colouring of
original works of art often
inspires interesting choices
of shades in yarn.*

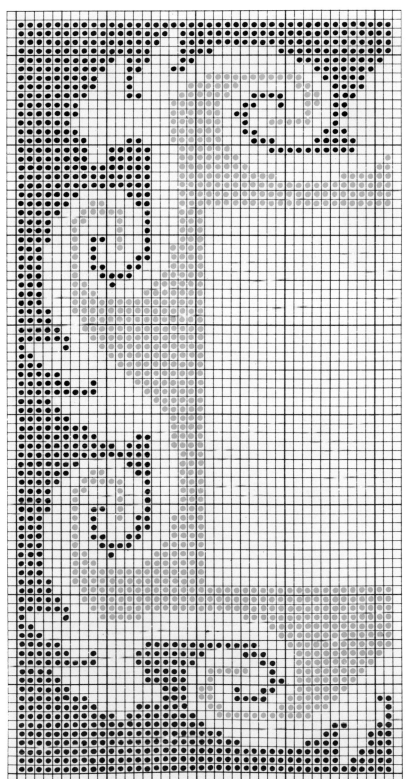

centre

43

**Ribbon Border**

| | |
|---|---|
| ◉ | 580 |
| ◎ | 582 |
| ⊟ | 583 |
| ◉ | 950 |
| ⋀ | 953 |
| ◉ | 951 |
| ☐ | 750 |
| ⋀ | 743 |
| · | 745 |

**Calculating Yarn Amounts:**
See page 121.
**Canvas requirements:** To
make a belt 91cms/36ins by
7.5cms/3ins you will need
107cms/42ins by 23cms/9ins
of 10 holes to the inch mesh.
The basic pattern will be
repeated five times – the
two-flower repeat is
18cms/7ins long.

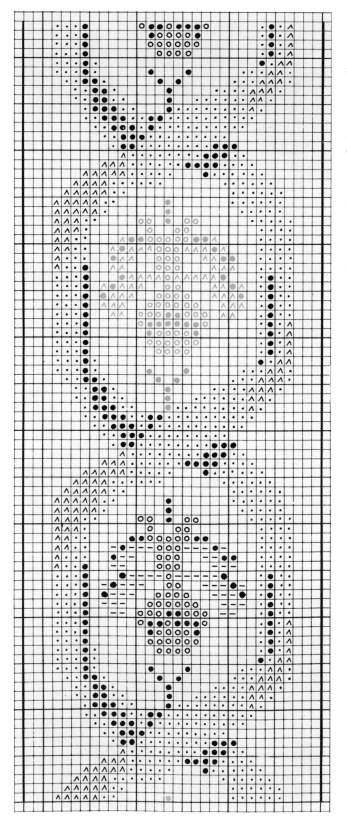

These borders – left and
overleaf – show how fine
work can be adapted for
needlepoints with some of
the character of the original.
The wave border, in fact,
becomes an interesting
exercise in colour balance,
which would create a very
different effect if the central
area were to be embroidered
in a dark colour, with two
lighter backgrounds either
side of it. It could be
combined with other designs
in the book for a striking
larger cushion cover:
perhaps the Burghley
flowers could be centred in
it, or the Chastleton rose.

# ELIZABETHAN SHELDON TAPESTRY

## Sudeley Castle

Sudeley Castle lies in the rich soft countryside of Gloucestershire; the ancient Romans had a settlement here at Belas Knap, and the Saxons used nearby Winchcombe as their capital in the 8th and 9th centuries. Its pedigree is ancient, and very distinguished.

Sudeley became the property of King Ethelred ('the Unready'), who came to enjoy deer hunting, and valued its large oak forest (trees then being a measure of worth in the way that olive trees still are in the Mediterranean). Ethelred's daughter inherited the land, as did her son, Ralph de Sudeley, a crusader knight. The present castle was built by one Boteler, Admiral of the Fleet under the Henrys V and VI. He became Baron Sudeley in 1441, but, unluckily for him, the tide turned with the Wars of the Roses, and he was forced to sell the Castle to Edward IV in 1469. It continued to be the home of royalty when Katharine Parr, the only wife of Henry VIII to outlive him, remarried Thomas Seymour, Lord High Admiral of England and Baron of Sudeley. A love letter written to her husband is kept at the Castle. Sadly, his affections had waned by the time she arrived at Sudeley with Lady Jane Grey in her retinue. Katharine died in childbirth, and Lady Jane Grey was beheaded after her unsuccessful bid for the throne.

Queen Elizabeth visited the Castle several times, but with the coming of the Civil War, its favoured life came to an end. Lord Chandos, then owner, defected to the Parliamentarian side. Sudeley, for a while, became a Roundhead garrison, and was eventually in large part demolished to prevent it ever becoming a Royalist stronghold again.

It was not until two wealthy glove manufacturers, the Dent brothers from nearby Worcester, bought the ruins in 1837 that Sudeley revived. They set about a massive rebuilding programme. Their nephew inherited much work in progress, and it is due to the work of his wife, Emma Brocklehurst, that the Castle was truly reborn. The Castle has remained in the family ever since.

For all its royal and political connections, Sudeley contains local treasures, many due to Emma Dent's assiduous collecting of items associated with the Castle's past. Among these is a famous tapestry made by Ralph Sheldon in about 1611 at his factory in Warwickshire. The weaving factory had been started at Barcheston in 1561 by William Sheldon in an effort to provide an alternative to expensive foreign imports, and to provide work for the local poor. The tapestries at Sudeley were undoubtedly the finest made in England at that time, and stand up to comparison with the more well-known European works of the period. They depict 'the Expulsion from Paradise', but this is merely an excuse to display all the glories of a Garden of Eden in a uniquely English context. Mythical beasts vie with the very English columbine, daffodil, foxglove, primula and lupin in richness of colour and detail. The serious religious theme is confined to medallion shapes against this mosaic-like background. A border of Elizabethan country scenes emphasizes the secular splendour of the wall-hanging, from which we have charted two details. Any one corner of the Sudeley tapestry is a feast for the eyes, and a reminder of the vigour and peculiarly English brilliance of the period in which it was made.

Bog irises from the Sudeley tapestry exemplify the realistic beauty of the work, the colour of which retains enough brilliance to suggest its former glory.

One small medallion from the Sudeley tapestry, made at the famous English Sheldon factory, reveals the sumptuous intricacy of the whole piece (shown overleaf).

The Sudeley tapestry in its entirety is a sumptuous display of flora and fauna; amongst the serious subjects based on the theme of 'The Expulsion from Paradise' lies a wealth of contemporary detail, like these scenes of hunting dogs and partridge and flowers. The chart (overleaf) derived from the hunting picture could be made into a cushion or a picture. The colours of the original are too appropriate to inspire alteration!

49

## Hunting Scene

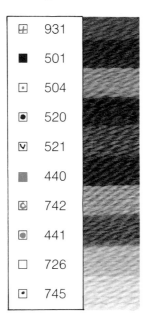

| | |
|---|---|
| ⊞ | 931 |
| ■ | 501 |
| ⊡ | 504 |
| ◉ | 520 |
| ☑ | 521 |
| ▦ | 440 |
| ◎ | 742 |
| ◉ | 441 |
| ☐ | 726 |
| ⊡ | 745 |

**Calculating Yarn Amounts:**
See page 121.
**Canvas requirements:** To
make a cushion or picture
40cms/16ins by 30cms/12ins
you will need 56cms/22ins by
46cms/18ins of 10 holes to
the inch mesh.

A detail from the Sudeley Sheldon tapestry exemplifies the vivid, tactile pleasure of the woven work. The authenticity of the floral designs is one of its chief qualities. Sheldon tapestries, woven in Barcheston, Gloucestershire, in the late 16th century are considered the finest English products of their age, and stand comparison with European ateliers.

53

## Heron and Flowers

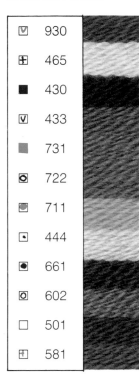

| | |
|---|---|
| ☑ | 930 |
| ⊞ | 465 |
| ■ | 430 |
| ☑ | 433 |
| ■ | 731 |
| ◉ | 722 |
| ▣ | 711 |
| ⊡ | 444 |
| ◉ | 661 |
| ◎ | 602 |
| □ | 501 |
| ⊞ | 581 |

**Calculating Yarn Amounts:**
See page 121.
**Canvas requirements:** To
make a picture or cushion
which is 46cms/16ins square
you will need 56cms/22ins
square of 10 holes to the inch
mesh.

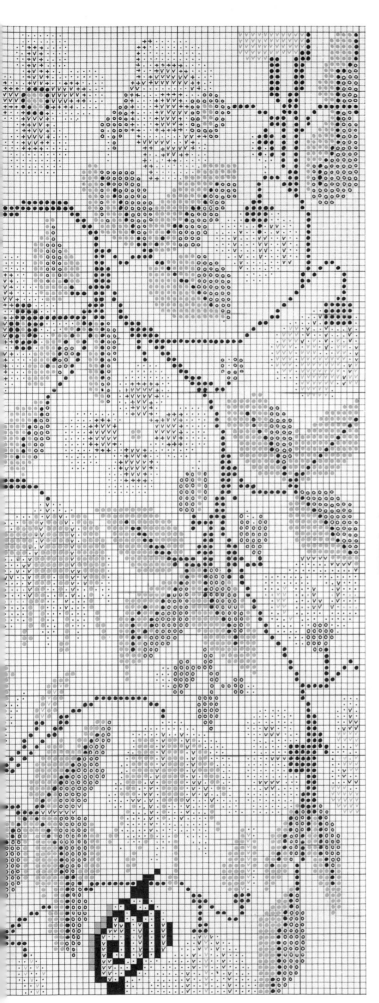

*Reproduced in colours inspired by the original tapestry, the Heron and Flowers project (left) is a detail from the country scenes depicting contemporary Jacobean pastimes among the aristocracy. The chart can be used to make a favourite cushion cover, but is fine enough to merit framing as a picture.*

# ANTIQUE SOFAS
## Burghley House

Burghley House is a magnificent palace, with romantic turrets and castellations. It is one of the grandest of Elizabethan edifices in the country, quite befitting its maker, William Cecil, first Lord Burghley, Treasurer to Queen Elizabeth I and one of the most powerful political figures of that time. His descendants have lived here, near the village of Burghley, in Lincolnshire, from which he took his title, ever since. His younger son, Robert, was created Earl of Salisbury and founded another dynasty, the Cecils of Hatfield.

Made of local limestone, a soft yellow that glows in sunshine, Burghley's exterior has not been altered much since its construction between 1555 and 1587. But the interior speaks more of 17th-century taste and the house contains so many fine objects that space permits mention of only a few: paintings by Veronese, Van Dyck, Gainsborough, Breughel; Gobelin tapestries, whose colourings still astonish; Grinling Gibbons carvings, Piranesi marbles, oriental porcelain and lacquered furniture, and many other treasures.

The rooms themselves contain history. A state bed covered in the most exquisite embroidery, recently restored, recalls a visit of Queen Elizabeth I. Another stateroom holds a bed worked in crewel stitch dating from the Queen Anne period and was used by King George VI and Queen Elizabeth, the Queen Mother, when Duke and Duchess of York. Two Soho tapestries also hang in this room, made by the royal tapestry maker John Vanderbanc at the time he moved to workrooms in Great Queen Street, London.

The furniture in one of the sitting rooms was gilded for a visit of Queen Victoria in 1844. The needlepoint designs were once thought to be the work of Hannah Sophia Chambers, wife of the 8th Earl of Exeter in the 18th century, but are more likely to be 19th-century work. The sofa featured here is related to the chairs in the subject matter of the flowers, but the treatment given them is quite different. While the chairs have the realism of embroideries influenced by the Dutch flower painters of the late 17th and early 18th centuries (part of the influx of all things Dutch under the reign of William and Mary), the sofa itself is worked with bolder, simplified versions, harking back to the earlier 17th-century tradition of crewel work with its stylized flowers often inspired by Oriental chintzes.

The cherub and vineleaf picture is adapted from a large sofa currently placed in the Old Ballroom. The sofa cover bears the monogram 'ED', that of Elizabeth, Countess of Devonshire, and was partly embroidered by her as a gift for her daughter Ann on her marriage to the 5th Earl of Exeter in 1670. It is therefore a piece of some age and rarity although the sofa itself is 19th century. The original work was possibly intended as a wall-hanging and cut down later to make a furnishing textile. Its width suggests it was not made as a bedhanging, nor is it the shape of a table cover.

Burghley House is also remembered in more recent times as the seat of the 6th Marquess, Lord Burghley, a noted sportsman and athlete who did much floor sport in the UK after the Second World War. His victory in the 400 metres hurdles at the 1928 Olympic Games in Amsterdam made him internationally famous, and was recalled in the film *Chariots of Fire*.

Two cherubs, surrounded by Bourbon roses and English Imperial lilies adorn the rare tapestry partly worked by the Countess of Devonshire at Burghley in 1670.

This sofa was gilded for Queen Victoria's visit to Burghley House. It displays the vigour of 19th-century taste in its bright colour and bold pattern.

**Floral Sofa**

**Calculating Yarn Amounts:**
See page 121.
**Canvas requirements:** To
make a long stool cover
61cms/24ins by 30cms/12ins
you will need 76cms/30ins by
46cms/18ins of 10 holes to
the inch mesh.

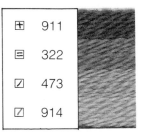

| | |
|---|---|
| ⊞ | 911 |
| ⊟ | 322 |
| ⊘ | 473 |
| ⊿ | 914 |

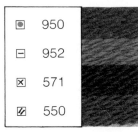

| | |
|---|---|
| ⊙ | 950 |
| ⊖ | 952 |
| ⊠ | 571 |
| ⊿ | 550 |

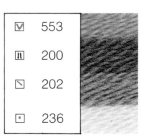

| | |
|---|---|
| ☑ | 553 |
| Ⅱ | 200 |
| ◺ | 202 |
| ⊡ | 236 |

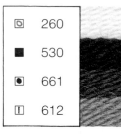

| | |
|---|---|
| ◨ | 260 |
| ■ | 530 |
| ◉ | 661 |
| ⊞ | 612 |

| | |
|---|---|
| ☒ | 663 |
| ⊡ | 712 |
| ☒ | 714 |
| ⧅ | 772 |

| | |
|---|---|
| ⧅ | 702 |
| ☒ | 700 |
| □ | 731 |

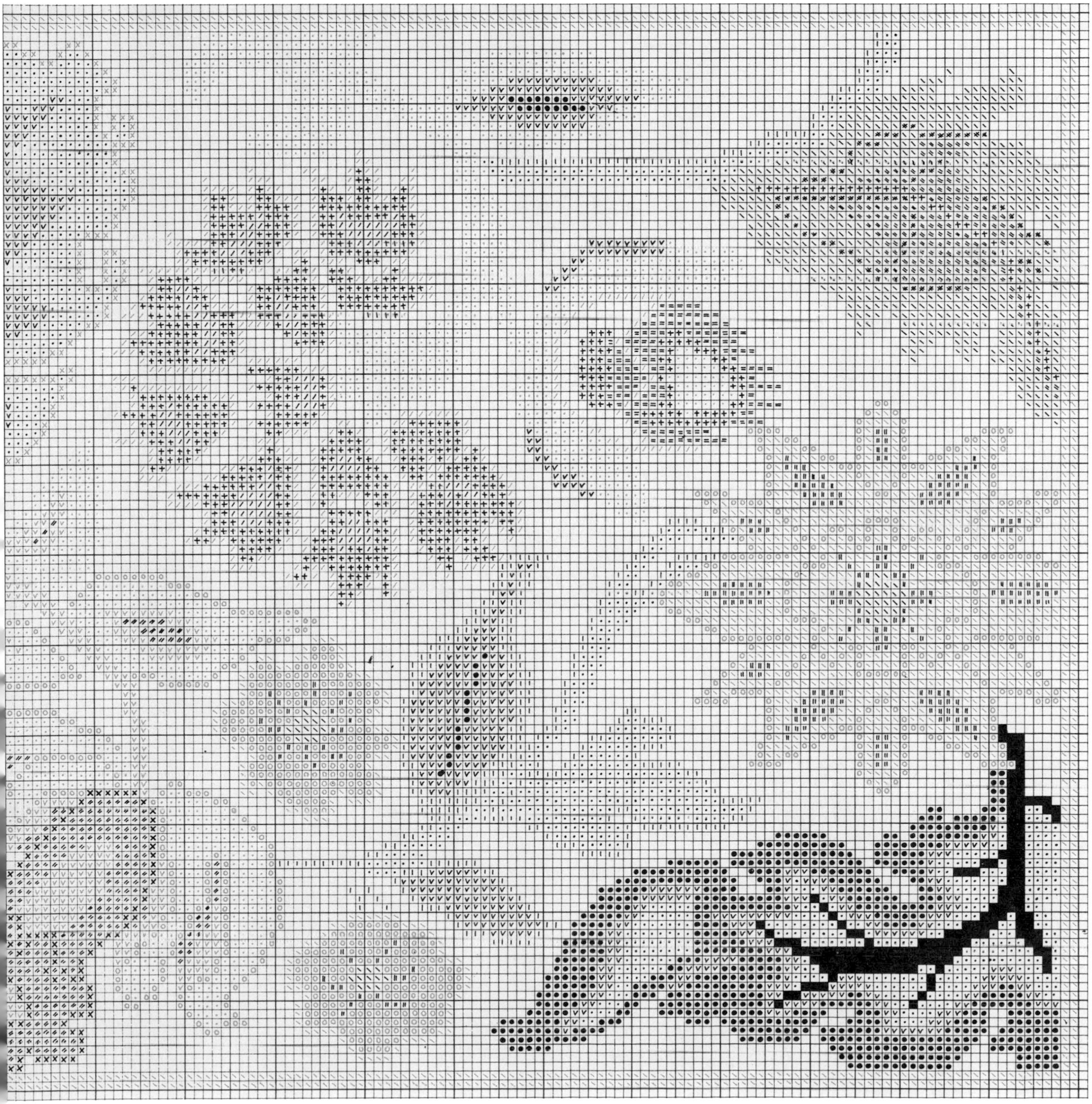

An enormous 19th-century sofa in the ballroom at Burghley House is covered in a much older piece of needlework, bearing the monogram of Elizabeth Countess of Devonshire, 1654-1700. The ribbon binding just visible is part of the remaking; the material may have been used as a wallhanging in its original state.

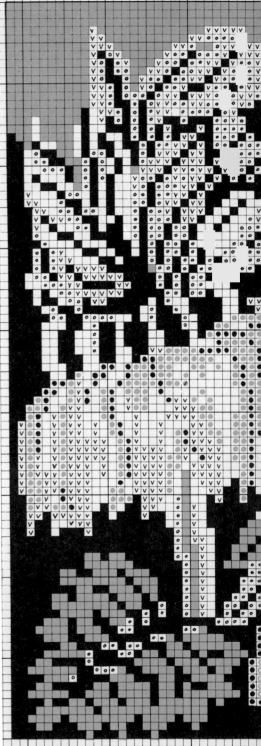

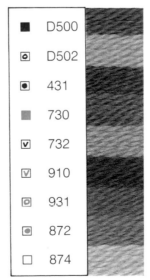

*The cherub sofa inspired this romantically coloured picture (above) – a beautiful gift for a special person.*

**Cherub Sofa**
**Calculating Yarn Amounts:**
See page 121.
**Canvas requirements:** To make a picture 23cms/9ins by 17cms/6½ins you will need 38cms/15ins by 30cms/12ins of 14 holes to the inch mesh.

| | |
|---|---|
| ■ | D500 |
| ◉ | D502 |
| ◉ | 431 |
| ■ | 730 |
| ☑ | 732 |
| ☑ | 910 |
| ◉ | 931 |
| ◉ | 872 |
| □ | 874 |

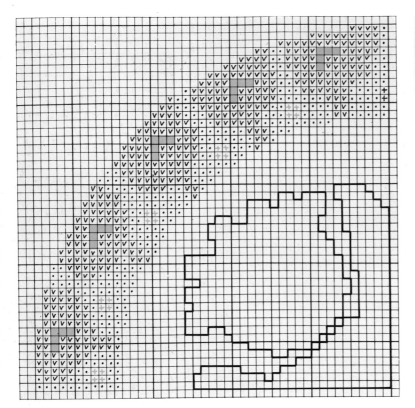

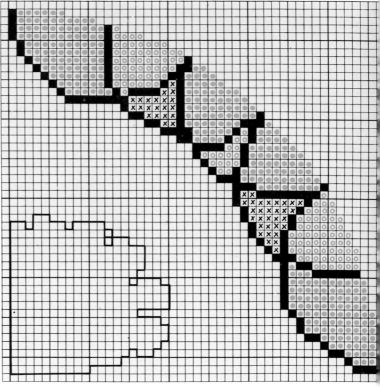

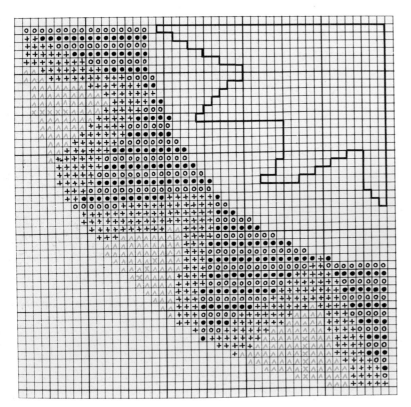

*These pretty flower heads are taken from the Burghley sofa (see chart on pages 58-9 for exact stitchery) and new borders have been designed to encircle them. Make them into round cushion centres, little decorative mats or small round purses with quilted backs.*

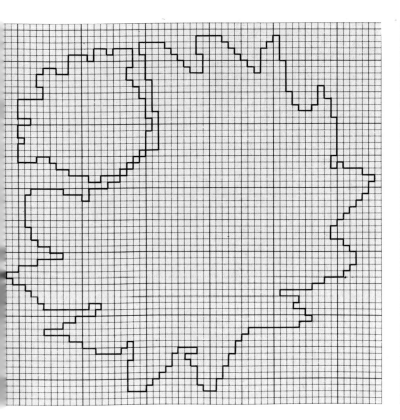

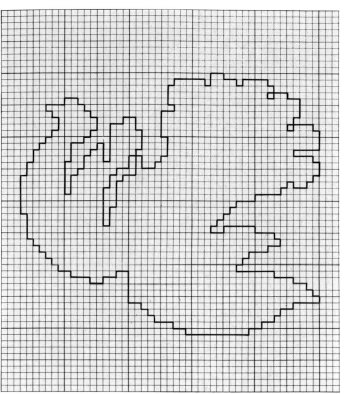

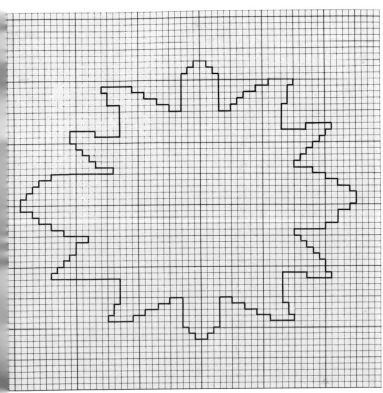

## Floral Details
**Calculating Yarn Amounts:** See page 121.
**Canvas requirements:** To make each small cushion or mat you will need 40cms/16ins diameter of 10 holes to the inch mesh.

### Bluebell

| | |
|---|---|
| ■ | 571 |
| ⊠ | 312 |
| ⊙ | 550 |
| ◉ | 553 |

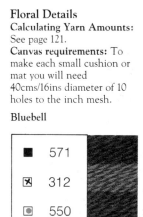

### Grey Flower

| | |
|---|---|
| ⊡ | 553 |
| ⊙ | 200 |
| ◿ | 202 |
| ⊞ | 236 |
| ⊞ | 712 |

### Pineapple

| | |
|---|---|
| ⊡ | 473 |
| ☑ | 914 |
| ⊞ | 772 |
| ■ | 700 |

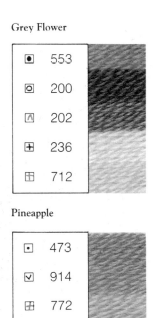

# WILLIAM MORRIS CUSHIONS
## Standen

Standen represents the Englishman's dream of a country house: late Victorian, comfortable with a modest degree of grandeur; set in folding hillsides with modest views of established gardens on all sides, and filled with rich textiles, good wood floors, and a generous light from tall windows. Many details of its architecture are imitated in lesser form by present-day interior decorators, but it has to be admitted that the larger scale of Standen makes attempts at copies poor in comparison. The architect was Philip Webb, a lifelong friend and colleague of William Morris, artist, poet, social reformer, who transformed taste in interiors at the end of the last century. Standen is the only major Webb house to survive intact. It was built in 1891-2 towards the end of his career, and conveys the essence of his and Morris' ideas – far from the 'greenery-yallery' criticism often levelled at the Arts and Crafts Movement. They believed a high standard of craftsmanship would produce good art and architecture, rather than a conscious borrowing of period styles, debased by commercialism and mass production.

The house was planned as a modest weekend retreat for a large London-based family and sited adjoining a much older building, the 'home-farm' of the property. This tile-hung structure influenced the architect, so that Standen has a modest exterior. But inside it is rich indeed, filled with beautiful 'Art Furnishings' (some from Morris' own firm), embroideries, ceramics of all styles, hand-woven carpets, and a great collection of original Morris wallpapers and textiles. The most characteristic colour used in the decoration (particularly the painted wood wall panelling) is a soft blue green – part of the palette used for the hand-woven, Morris-designed cushions chosen here. They are symmetrical, and make great use of colours of close tone – a style much favoured by Morris in his work.

Any embroiderer visiting the house would find years of inspiration for their craft. Many of the William de Morgan tiles lend themselves perfectly to execution in canvaswork. In the hall is an embroidery of Morris' 'Vine' pattern, executed by Margaret Beale, the wife of the owner. There is a portrait of her by Sir William Nicholson, in which she wears a Pre-Raphaelite loose robe, and concentrates on her knitting, indicating her enthusiasm for handicrafts.

Several rooms of the house contain needlepoint cushions worked by members of the family. The dining room, most beautifully panelled and painted soft green, is filled with Chinese blue and white porcelain, and contains original Morris tapestry curtains in his 'Peacock and Dragon' design. The dining chairs, a complete set with chintz needlepoint seats, each varied with a mythical beast in the centre, were also made by the family over a period up to the 1920s. As is common in earlier 18th-century pieces, the borders of stylized leaves are in *gros point*, and the central motifs in *petit point*.

Margaret Beale also took charge of the garden, which was left very much as she had created it when the house was given to the National Trust in 1972 by her daughter Helen. Not as simply 'natural' as the architect would have perhaps wanted, but filled with brightly coloured and unusual plants, the garden adds to the general impression of a much-loved home for a creative family.

The stylized sunflower on the Standen woven cushion cover, a favourite motif of William Morris, which has been transformed into a needlepoint chart.

The billiard room at Standen shows how every detail of the interior was chosen to create harmony: a wonderful setting for Morris' timeless designs.

William Morris' genius in pattern and colouring are well known, and through the continuing popularity of his designs, alternative colourways for his designs suggest themselves quite readily. Ochres and deep reds were chosen because they remind us of the interest in hand-made objects, wood and ceramic, that Morris promoted. Colour schemes based on nature's combinations are in sympathy with the stylized flower shapes.

### Sunflower Cushion
**Alternative colours**

- ◉ 730
- ● 732
- ☐ 735
- ☑ 562

**Original colours**

- ☐ 500
- ◉ 611
- ☑ 930
- ◉ 913

**Calculating Yarn Amounts:** See page 121.

**Canvas requirements:** To make a 41cm/16in square cushion you will need 56cms/22ins square of 10 holes to the inch mesh.

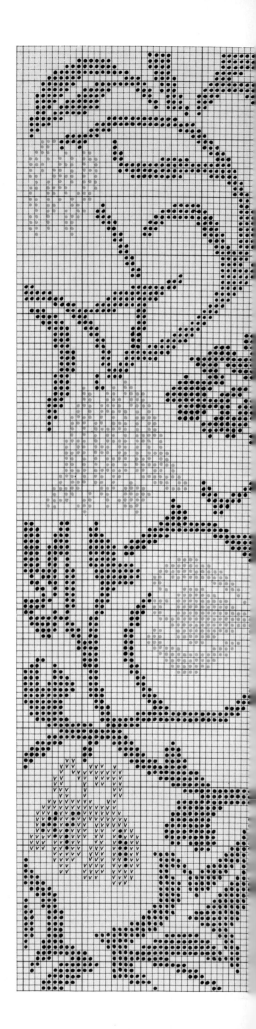

## Orange Tree Cushion

**Calculating Yarn Amounts:**
See page 121.
**Canvas requirements:** To
make a cushion 43cms/17ins
by 41cms/16ins you will need
59cms/23ins by 56cms/22ins
of 10 holes to the inch mesh.

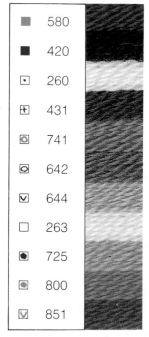

| | |
|---|---|
| ■ | 580 |
| ■ | 420 |
| ⊡ | 260 |
| ⊞ | 431 |
| ◎ | 741 |
| ◎ | 642 |
| ☑ | 644 |
| ☐ | 263 |
| ◉ | 725 |
| ◑ | 800 |
| ☑ | 851 |

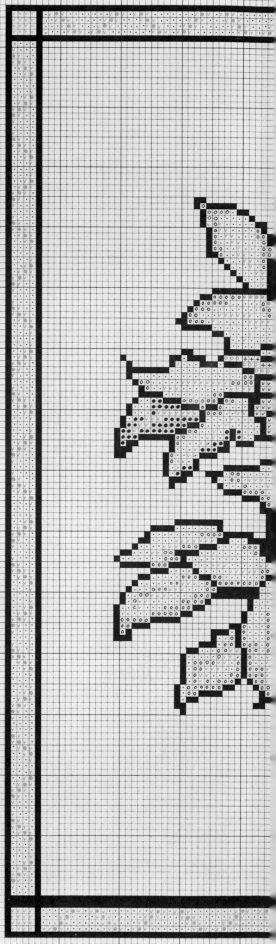

centre

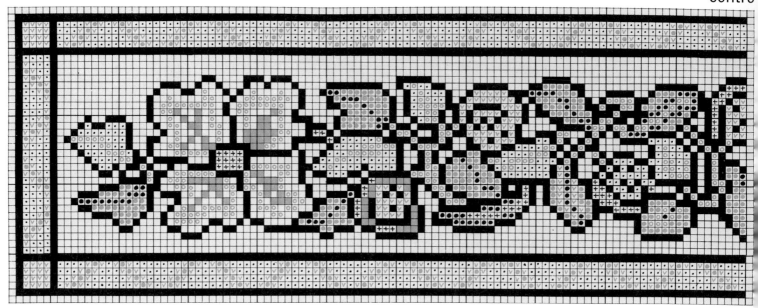

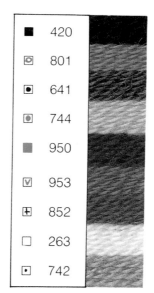

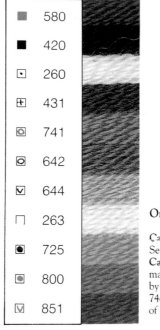

| | |
|---|---|
| ■ | 580 |
| ■ | 420 |
| ⊡ | 260 |
| ⊞ | 431 |
| ◎ | 741 |
| ◒ | 642 |
| ☑ | 644 |
| ☐ | 263 |
| ◉ | 725 |
| ◉ | 800 |
| ☑ | 851 |

| | |
|---|---|
| ■ | 420 |
| ◙ | 801 |
| ◙ | 641 |
| ◉ | 744 |
| ■ | 950 |
| ☑ | 953 |
| ⊞ | 852 |
| ☐ | 263 |
| ⊡ | 742 |

### Orange Tree Tie-back

**Calculating Yarn Amounts:**
See page 121.
**Canvas requirements:** To
make a curtain tie-back
54cms/21ins by 10cms/4ins
you will need 69cms/27ins by
25cms/10ins of 10 holes to
the inch mesh.

### Orange Tree Bolster

**Calculating Yarn Amounts:**
See page 121.
**Canvas requirements:** To
make a bolster 59cms/23ins
by 20cms/8ins you will need
74cms/29ins by 36cms/14ins
of 10 holes to the inch mesh.

*Detals from the Belton
House chair have been
charted and made into
attractive cushions and a
tie-back.*

# FLORENTINE-STITCHED CHAIRS
## Dorney Court

The beginning of the entry in the Domesday book referring to the manor of Dorney reads 'Terra Milonis Crispin'. Situated close to Windsor, an easy ride from London, the land would always have had value, and recent excavations show that there was a substantial manor house there in medieval times. By the 16th century, though, it belonged to the Lord Mayor of London, Sir William Gerrard. His daughter married Sir James Palmer of Kent, and from that time, the house has remained in the Palmer family.

It now stands close to modern life, a few miles from motorways and urban development, and yet retains an atmosphere of a prosperous Elizabethan home. Dorney Common nearby has not changed in 500 years and is still used by those with 'common rights'. Dorney Court itself is a magnificent late medieval, timber-framed building: a kingpin dates it as 1510, but the main timber frame dates from c.1440. The Great Hall is a fine example of Tudor architecture, with its high oak beams, linenfold panelling, and family portraits including previous owners of the house, Roger Palmer, the Earl, and his wife the Countess of Castelmaine, by Lely.

Not surprisingly, the Palmer family were monarchists. Sir James Palmer was Chancellor to Charles I, a Governor of the Mortlake tapestry factory, and a distinguished painter of miniatures, regarded in the same class as Nicholas Hilliard. His portrait hangs in the Great Hall but sadly his fine collection of miniatures was stolen by Cromwell's soldiers when they pillaged the house.

Another treasure lost from Dorney was fortunately recovered. An embroidery depicting the Palmer family tree, a combination of crewel and stumpwork, was made as a gift for Thomas Palmer's wedding in 1624 by a female relative, mother or grandmother. It depicts the Palmer triplets who – so legend relates – were born on three consecutive Sundays in 1489. Two of them became knights. Five other titled Palmers of the 16th century are also shown, with palm trees and other heraldic motifs. One of the rarest pieces of English embroidery, it was long thought to belong to the Earls of Winchelsea, until properly studied at the turn of this century when its real provenance was established. By this date it had found its way into the possession of Lord Northcliffe. In 1909, Wenna Palmer, wife of Colonel Charles Palmer who restored Dorney to its Tudor appearance, visited Sutton Place, Lord Northcliffe's home: 'there I found the long lost Palmer tapestry. I nearly screamed'. In 1910, the piece was handed back to the rightful owners, a generous gesture from Lord Northcliffe, to become a much-prized family heirloom. There are other rare pieces of embroidery in the panelled bedrooms of the house, including 17th-century Florentine flamestitch curtains, and appliquéd, stumpwork-like dancing figures on a cloth from the Andaman Islands.

Wenna Palmer was herself an embroiderer, as chairs in the drawing room of Dorney testify. It is a beautiful, comfortable room, octagonal in shape, with mullioned windows and a low, beamed ceiling – the oldest part of the house. Most of the furniture here is embroidered in a variety of Florentine stitch patterns; the red sofa was made by Wenna Palmer, but the grayish diamond patterned chairs are considerably older, European, and on a finer mesh of canvas.

One of several romantic knights from the Dorney Court stumpwork picture. It is a rare 17th-century family tree of the Palmers, who still live in the house.

The drawing rooms intact from its original date, 1510. Some original needlepoint covers are imports from Europe, and others are made by the family.

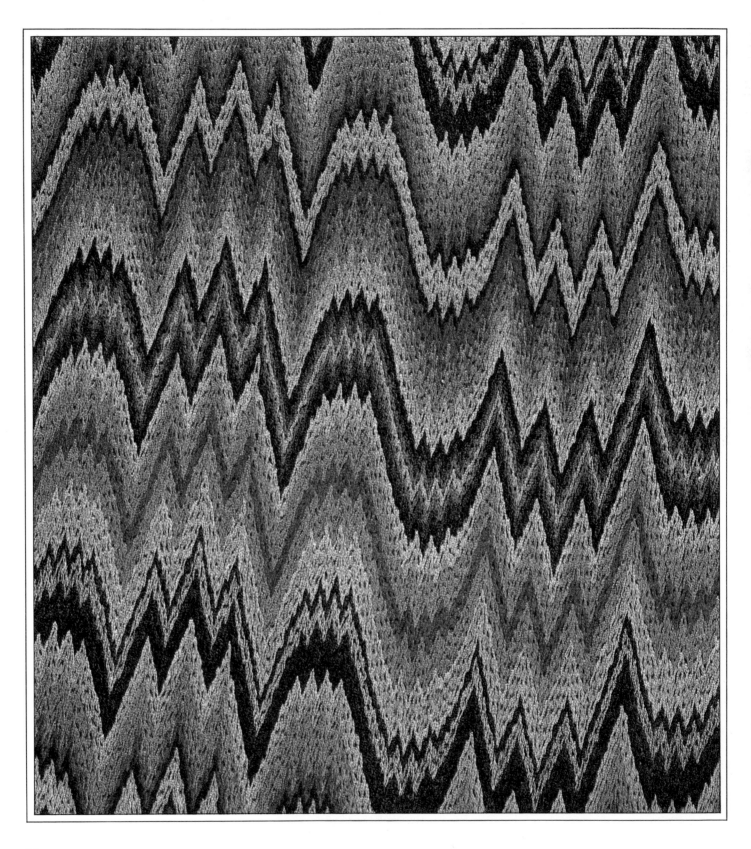

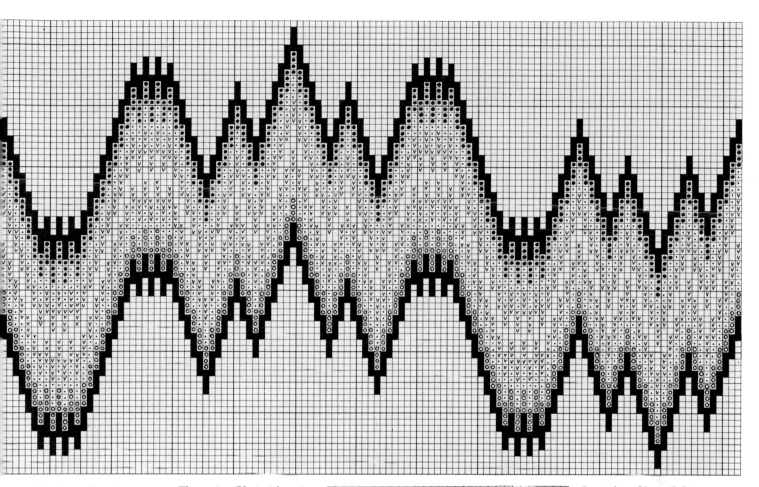

**Calculating Yarn Amounts:**
See page 121.
**Canvas requirements:** To
make a 33cms/13ins square
cushion you will need
48cms/19ins square of 10
holes to the inch mesh.

*Left: This detail from one
of the chairs at Dorney
Court shows how readily
the flame pattern lends itself
to colour experiment. Each
wave can be alternated with
a band of softer colour, like
the subtle oranges between
the blues and green shown
here – colours have been
suggested with the chart.
The chart is simply repeated
for each wave of colour you
create.*

**Florentine Chair** (above)

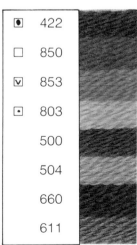

| | |
|---|---|
| ▣ | 422 |
| ☐ | 850 |
| ☑ | 853 |
| ⊡ | 803 |
| | 500 |
| | 504 |
| | 660 |
| | 611 |

*Above: The Leviathan
stitch, a sort of double cross
stitch, is found on the chair
bearing this simple,
patchwork-like design.*

**Leviathan Chair** (left)

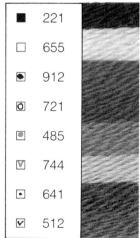

| | |
|---|---|
| ■ | 221 |
| ☐ | 655 |
| ▣ | 912 |
| ⊘ | 721 |
| ▣ | 485 |
| ☑ | 744 |
| · | 641 |
| ☑ | 512 |

**Calculating Yarn Amounts:** See page 121.
**Canvas requirements:** To make a 33cms/13ins
square cushion you will need 48cms/19ins square of
10 holes to the inch mesh.

# BED DRAPES AND FLORAL SCREEN
## Blair Castle

Blair Castle in Perthshire is the home of the Dukes of Atholl, and presents the visitor with stunning vistas of high, white-harled walls, castellated towers and blue-grey turreted rooftops. Surrounded by the forests of Atholl and the Banvie burn close by, the Castle speaks of its past as a fortress – strategically placed on the main route through the central highlands – and also, since the 13th century, its distinction as a nobleman's home.

Sir John Stewart of Balvenie, King James II's maternal half-brother and ancestor of the present Atholl family, was conferred the earldom in 1457. During the Civil War, the then Earl was an ardent Royalist who died in 1642, and, in 1652, the Castle was held by Cromwell's troops until the Restoration. The Earl's son, the 1st Marquis of Atholl, married Lady Amelia Stanley, daughter of the 7th Earl of Derby, who may have influenced him in his decision to support William of Orange (her cousin), and not to take part in the last great battle in support of King James – the Battle of Killiecrankie in 1689. When England and Scotland were finally united, the Marquis' posthumous reward was to have his own son created the first Duke of Atholl in 1703.

This brief glance into Blair's history adds some resonance to the choice of embroideries from the Castle. The ornate, beautifully coloured fish are part of the 'slips' (individually needlepointed motifs, cut out and appliquéd to finer fabrics), made at a time of great political crisis. Lady Amelia Stanley's mother, Charlotte de Trémouille, was herself besieged during the Civil War at Latham House (in England, now destroyed), and made the embroideries for her daughter. The satin bedhangings that now adorn the late 18th-century four-poster are dotted with naïve animals, swags of bright flowers, and colourful little birds. If ever there was evidence of the calming influence of needlecraft, then these lively, brilliant designs reveal its power.

Blair Castle is filled with other fine examples of the art of embroidery. A small drawing room on the first floor contains a set of mahogany chairs from the Queen Anne period, noteworthy for the 'fish-scale' patterning carved all over their legs. The seat covers were made by Jean Drummond, the 2nd Duke of Atholl's wife, whom he married in 1749. They depict a cornucopia, filled on each chair with different flowers – primulas, carnations, iris, tulips and roses. Incidentally, the set of eight chairs was delivered in 1756 on the payment of the princely sum of £26.10s.

Jean Drummond also worked the firescreen chosen for this collection, found in the bedroom at Blair called the Derby room. Part of its charm lies in the almost Japanese, certainly painterly quality that the fading of the stitchery has produced – although the cause is pure science. Early natural dyestuffs contained chemicals that, over a period of time, literally eat up fibres as they oxidize in the air. The original background may have been uniformly dark, and the foreground colours much more brilliant; greens in particular fade to a muted blue with age. But its present condition is pleasing, whatever the defects, and the background could be simulated by leaving areas of the canvas blank, or by painting on it with fabric dyes. Alternatively, a background could be worked in a finer silk thread than the tapestry wool used for the flowers.

This wild boar – a sturdy, credible little animal – is but one of the many delights of the Blair bedhangings. The original needlework is on an impressively fine scale.

The sumptuous satin hangings of Blair Castle, richly covered in needlepoint appliqué 'slips' depicting flower swags, adventurers and mythical creatures.

84

The colouring of this fish at Blair Castle is so subtle that the shapes seem alive. They demonstrate that needlework can be a fine art, with a unique tactile quality.

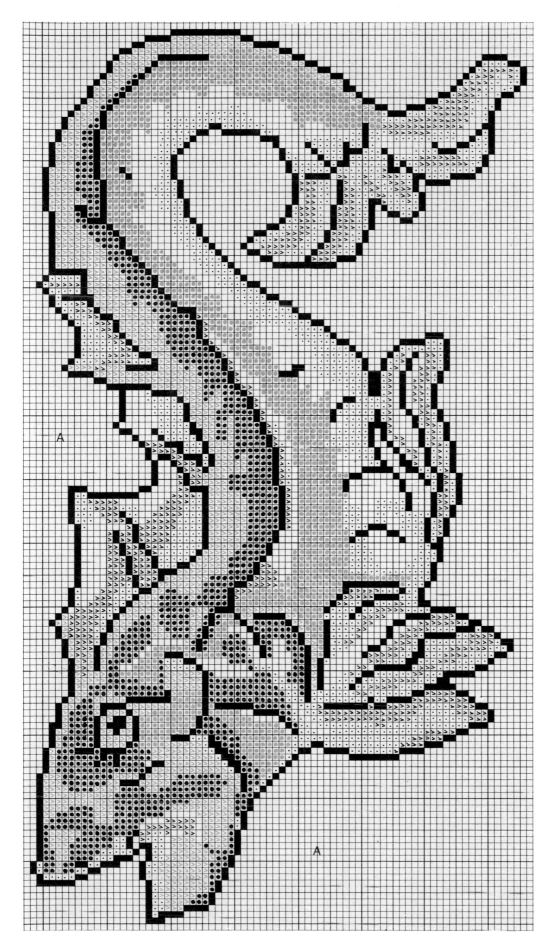

## Swimming Fish

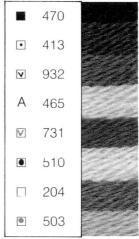

| | |
|---|---|
| ■ | 470 |
| ⊡ | 413 |
| ☑ | 932 |
| A | 465 |
| ☑ | 731 |
| ◉ | 510 |
| ☐ | 204 |
| ◉ | 503 |

**Calculating Yarn Amounts:**
See page 121.
**Canvas requirements:** To make a cushion 38cms/15ins by 23cms/9ins you will need 53cms/21ins by 38cms/15ins of 10 holes to the inch mesh.

centre

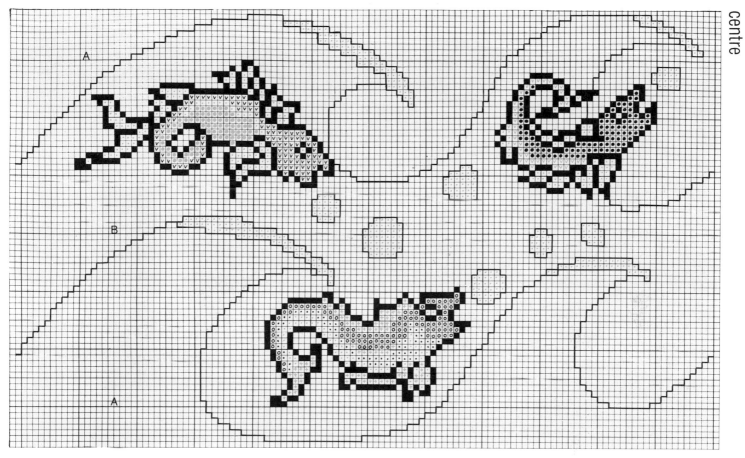

## Serpent Fish (left)

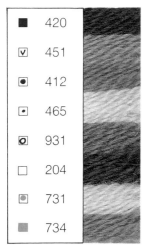

| | |
|---|---|
| ■ | 420 |
| ☑ | 451 |
| ◉ | 412 |
| ⊡ | 465 |
| ◎ | 931 |
| □ | 204 |
| ◉ | 731 |
| ▦ | 734 |

**Calculating Yarn Amounts:**
See page 121.
**Canvas requirements:** To
make a cushion 36cms/14ins
by 30cms/12ins you will need
50cms/20ins by 46cms/18ins
of 10 holes to the inch mesh.

## Fish Rug (above)

| | |
|---|---|
| ⊡ | 561 |
| ☑ | 541 |
| ◉ | 543 |
| A | 582 |
| B | 584 |
| ■ | 530 |
| ◎ | 692 |
| ☑ | 732 |
| ⊞ | 932 |
| ▱ | 263 |
| ◉ | 401 |

**Calculating Yarn Amounts:**
See page 121.
**Canvas requirements:** To
make this rug you will need
137cms/54ins by 96cms/38ins
of 5 holes to the inch mesh.

*The fish have been worked
together against a wave
pattern to make a rug;
aquamarines and blues give
the fish a jewel-like
brilliance against a receding
ground.*

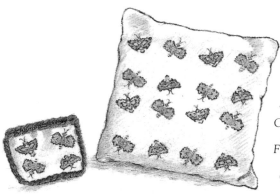

*The tiny butterflies dotted on the slips at Blair Castle (left) are so finely detailed that they have been conceived in two forms for needlepoint. First, for a cushion cover, and second on a finer scale as a motif for brooches. The firescreen (right), though faded, is still perfect enough to show the superb craft in its making.*

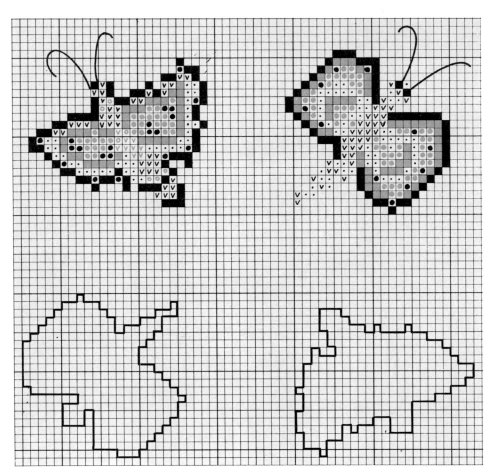

**Butterflies**

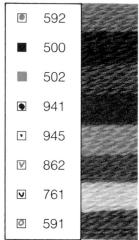

| | |
|---|---|
| ◉ | 592 |
| ■ | 500 |
| ▨ | 502 |
| ◉ | 941 |
| · | 945 |
| ☑ | 862 |
| ☑ | 761 |
| ◎ | 591 |

**Calculating Yarn Amounts:** See page 121.

**Canvas requirements:** Each butterfly uses approximately 3cms/1½ins square of canvas at 22 holes to the inch mesh if using as motifs for brooches. Should you wish to make the large cushion illustrated above, you will need 25cms/10ins square of 14 holes to the inch mesh; and for the small cushion, 13cms/5ins square.

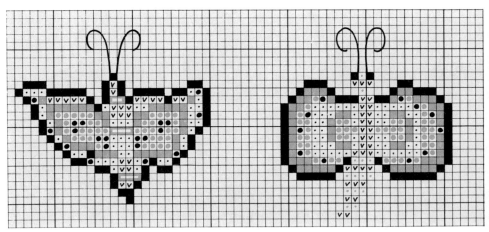

**Floral Screen**

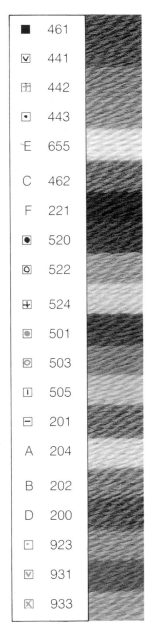

| | |
|---|---|
| ■ | 461 |
| ☑ | 441 |
| ⊞ | 442 |
| ⊡ | 443 |
| E | 655 |
| C | 462 |
| F | 221 |
| ◉ | 520 |
| ⊙ | 522 |
| ⊞ | 524 |
| ◉ | 501 |
| ⊙ | 503 |
| ⊡ | 505 |
| ⊟ | 201 |
| A | 204 |
| B | 202 |
| D | 200 |
| ⊡ | 923 |
| ☑ | 931 |
| ☒ | 933 |

**Calculating Yarn Amounts:**
See page 121.
**Canvas requirements:** To
make this screen or picture
you will need 61cms/24ins by
71cms/28ins of 14 holes to
the inch mesh.

## Floral Screen

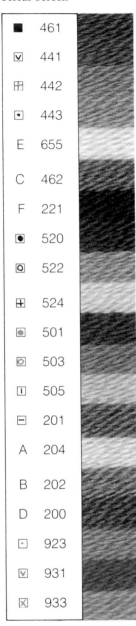

| | |
|---|---|
| ■ | 461 |
| ☑ | 441 |
| ⊞ | 442 |
| ⊡ | 443 |
| E | 655 |
| C | 462 |
| F | 221 |
| ◉ | 520 |
| ◎ | 522 |
| ⊞ | 524 |
| ◉ | 501 |
| ◎ | 503 |
| ⊡ | 505 |
| ⊟ | 201 |
| A | 204 |
| B | 202 |
| D | 200 |
| ⊡ | 923 |
| ☑ | 931 |
| ⊠ | 933 |

**Calculating Yarn Amounts:**
See page 121.
**Canvas requirements:** To
make this screen or picture
you will need 61cms/24ins by
71cms/28ins of 14 holes to
the inch mesh.

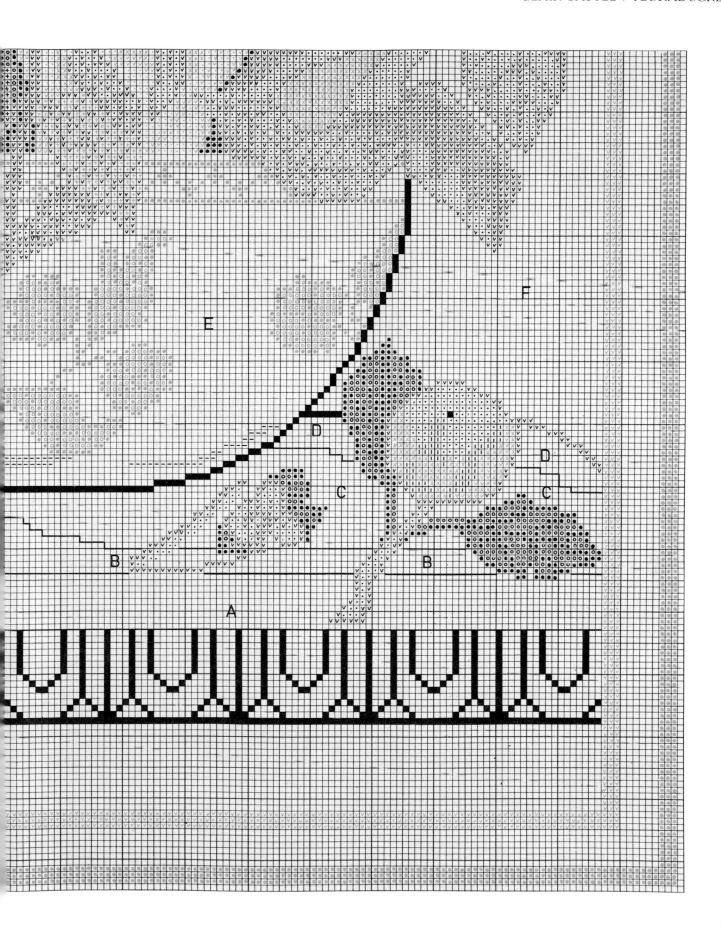

# A FLAME-STITCH ROOM AND TUDOR CUSHION

## Chastleton

Chastleton is a remarkable early Jacobean building which has hardly been altered since it was built in 1603 by Walter Jones, a rich wool stapler and a Member of Parliament. He bought the estate of Chastleton in Gloucestershire for £4,000 from Robert Catesby, a gunpowder plot conspirator along with Guy Fawkes, and Walter's son Henry and his wife Anne are among the ancestors of George Washington.

The house has a symmetrical beauty, with five gables and a tower at each side to hold the main staircases. There is a central courtyard and a Great Hall finely panelled with Jacobean carved wood; most of the interior woodwork is original. On the first floor of the house is the most impressive room of all: the Great Chamber, containing elaborately carved panelling stained a reddish colour, a magnificent chimneypiece and a plasterwork ceiling with numerous pendants, bringing an almost exotic splendour to the room.

It is perhaps not surprising to find a treasury of needlework in the home of a wool merchant: Walter Jones traded across England, and also France and Italy. Upstairs, the walls of a small closet, or dressing room, are covered from floor to ceiling with panels of Hungarian point flame pattern, identical to the important bedhangings to be seen at Parham Park in Sussex. The panelling and plasterwork in this room were designed to fit around the tapestry and it has been hanging in the house since it was built: listed in Walter Jones's inventory of chattels dated 1663, it is extremely rare and valuable. The colour gradations must have been exquisite when the silk and wool used were fresh; even with irregular fading (different dyed yarn batches changing colour variously) the effect is splendid.

The Jones family were Royalists; in the beautiful Long Gallery at the top of the house, where indoor games were played on wet days, Charles I's Bible is kept. This was the copy he read in prison, and gave to a bishop on the morning of his execution. When the bishop's family line came to an end in the 18th century, the Bible was handed on to the Jones', as known supporters of the monarch, for safekeeping.

After the Civil War Battle of Worcester, when Charles II was defeated, Arthur, grandson of the original owner of Chastleton, hid in a tiny secret room, the door of which is disguised as the back of a bedroom cupboard. Cromwell's soldiers came to the house in pursuit of him, and decided to spend the night in the very bedroom next to his hiding place. Arthur's wife Sarah put opium in their beer and when they fell into a drugged sleep he escaped on one of the enemies' best horses.

Such loyalist connections give life to the emblems of Tudor rose, hearts and barley-sugar twists embroidered on a long cushion cover at Chastleton. This dates from the 16th century and also contains a pomegranate central motif, repeated in the plasterwork of the room it decorates – a small bedroom adjoining the Great Chamber. The colours of the original were brilliant reds, blues, pinks and golds; as with many other faded embroideries, the authentic vivid hues are still visible on the reverse, preserved from air. Chastleton must have glowed with the richness of tapestry colours in its heyday.

The pomegranate motif originates in Byzantine art, but at Chastleton it is combined in needlepoint with the uniquely English Tudor rose and barley twist pattern.

A dressing room at Chastleton is intact with its many original 17th-century Hungarian point panels, entirely covering the walls and even the door.

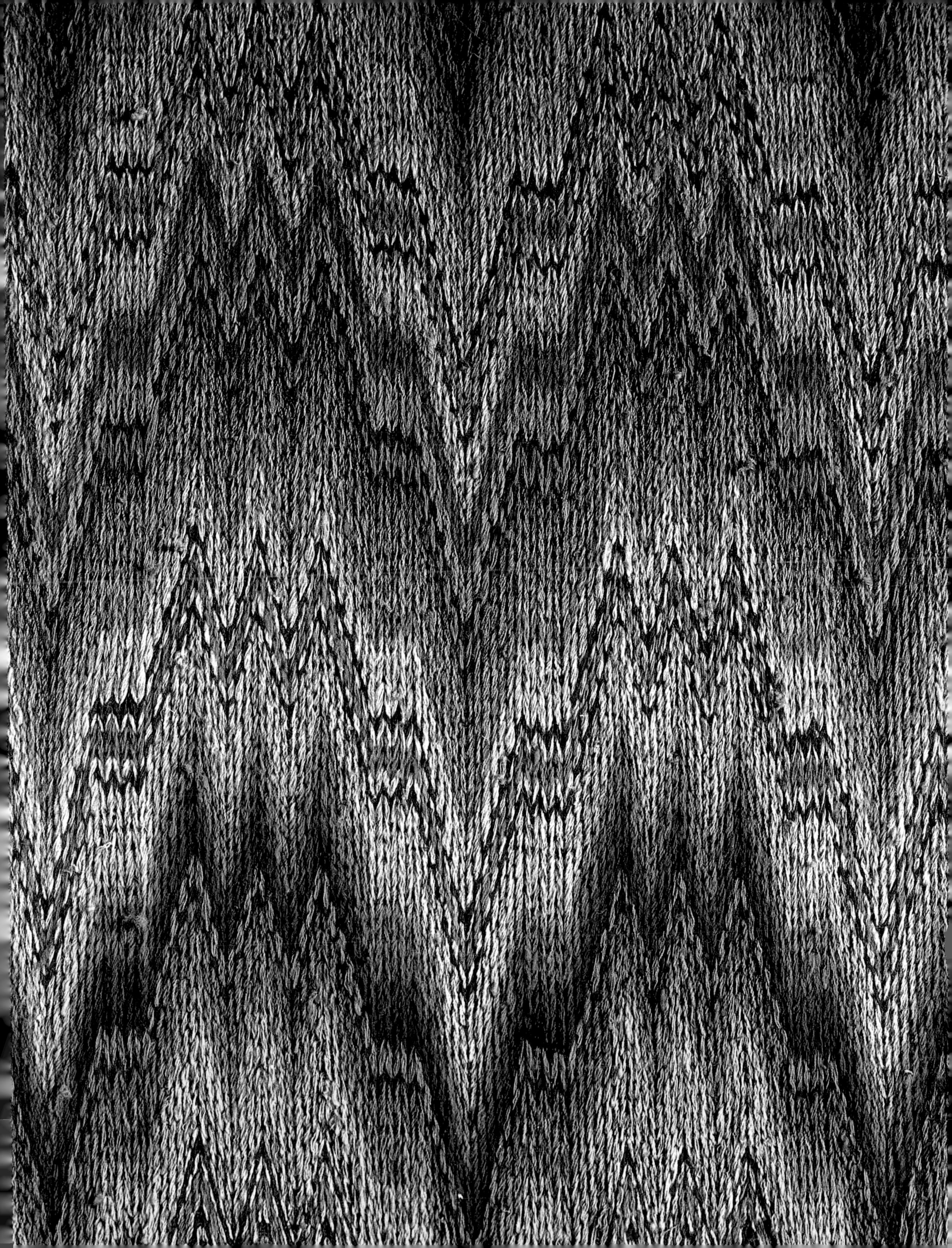

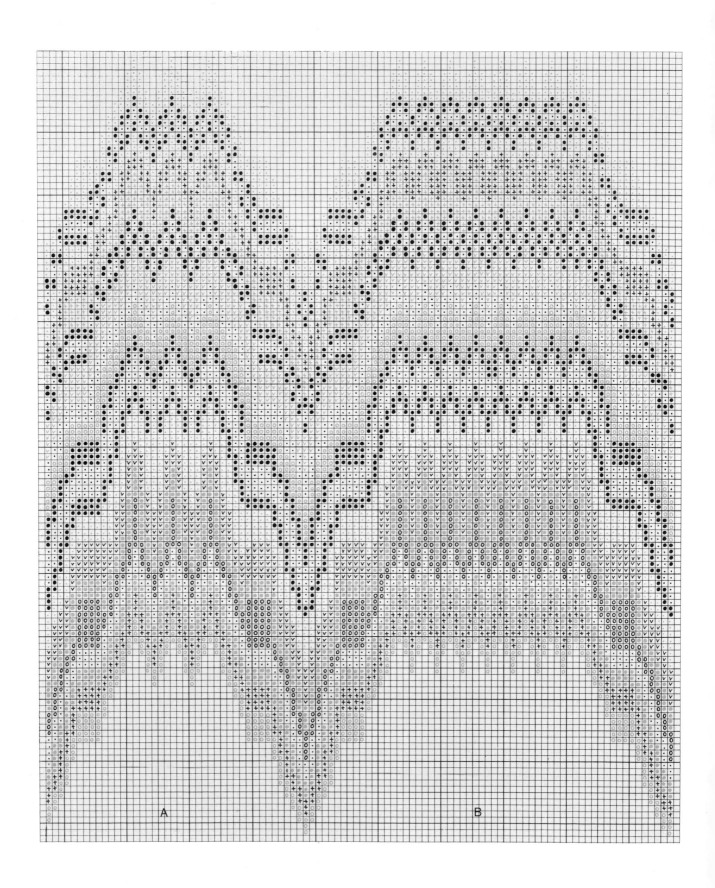

A                                          B

**Flame-stitch Pattern**

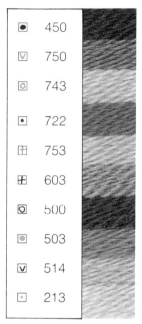

| | |
|---|---|
| ◉ | 450 |
| ⊻ | 750 |
| ◎ | 743 |
| ⊡ | 722 |
| ⊞ | 753 |
| ⊞ | 603 |
| ◙ | 500 |
| ◉ | 503 |
| ☑ | 514 |
| ⊡ | 213 |

**Calculating Yarn Amounts:**
See page 121.
**Canvas requirements:** To
make a jewelery roll
36cms/14ins by 22cms/8½ins
you will need 43cms/17ins by
28cms/11ins of 10 holes to
the inch mesh.

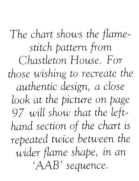

*The chart shows the flame-
stitch pattern from
Chastleton House. For
those wishing to recreate the
authentic design, a close
look at the picture on page
97 will show that the left-
hand section of the chart is
repeated twice between the
wider flame shape, in an
'AAB' sequence.*

Right: The original, 16th-century long cushion cover at Chastleton shows a stylized pomegranate surrounded by the popular Elizabethan 'barley sugar' motif, with Tudor roses at their intersections. The flower and the diamond framing were probably adapted from Italian brocade fabric, especially as the owner of Chastleton was a wool merchant who traded with European textile makers. The same design is found in various other colourways in the house.

This jewelery roll has been embroidered in the original colouring using just two 'AA' panels of the flame pattern.

## Tudor Long Cushion

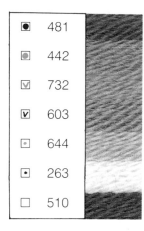

| | |
|---|---|
| ◉ | 481 |
| ◉ | 442 |
| ☑ | 732 |
| ☑ | 603 |
| ⊡ | 644 |
| ⊡ | 263 |
| ☐ | 510 |

**Calculating Yarn Amounts:**
See page 121.
**Canvas requirements:** To
make a cushion 30cms/12ins
by 35cms/14ins you will need
46cms/18ins by 50cms/20ins
of 10 holes to the inch mesh.

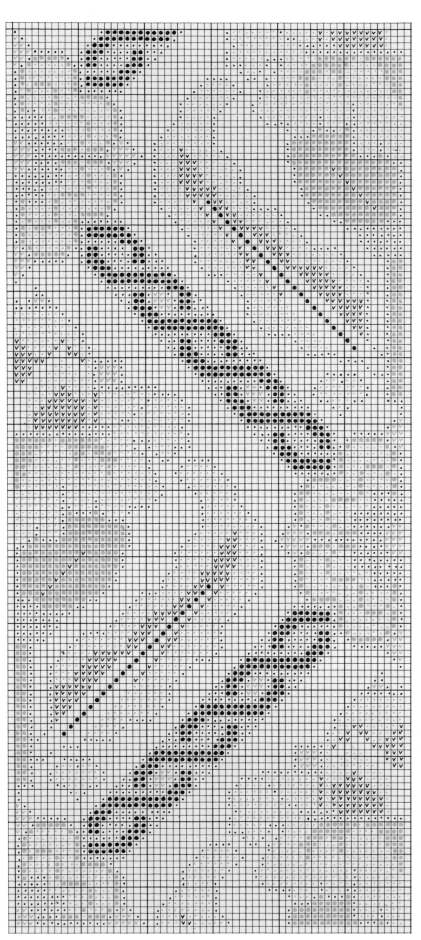

**Rose and Hearts
Cushions** (right)

**Calculating Yarn Amounts:**
See page 121.
**Canvas requirements:** To
make the cushions featured
on this page you will need
33cms/13ins by 36cms/14ins
of 10 holes to the inch mesh
for the smaller versions and
64cms/25ins by 66cms/26ins
for the larger one.

centre

**Large cushion**

| | |
|---|---|
| ◉ | 901 |
| ▨ | 952 |
| ◻ | 955 |
| ◐ | 948 |
| ☐ | 520 |
| ■ | 420 |
| ✓ | 711 |

**Small cushion**

| | |
|---|---|
| ✓ | 726 |
| ▬ | 470 |
| ☐ | 455 |
| ◐ | 703 |
| ▪ | 940 |
| ◻ | 944 |
| ▨ | 942 |

**Barley Twist cushion**

| | |
|---|---|
| ◉ | 970 |
| ◐ | 961 |
| ◻ | 963 |
| ▨ | 261 |
| ✓ | 580 |
| ■ | 220 |
| ☐ | 696 |
| ✓ | 760 |

# EIGHTEENTH-CENTURY RURAL SCENES
## Castle Ashby

Castle Ashby has an ancient history. Judith, niece of William the Conqueror, married Waltheof, Earl of Northampton, and was given several estates in the area of Ashby as part of her dowry. However, construction of the present house was only begun in 1574 by the Compton family who had purchased the land from the Earl of Kent in 1512. Family tradition claims that Queen Elizabeth once visited the house, and on three visits Lord Compton entertained King James in lavish style.

Early in the 17th century, Inigo Jones may have been employed at Castle Ashby on rebuilding work, for the architect in charge relates, he 'finished one front; but the Civil War put a stop to all Arts'. However, some of the building work was more likely under the charge of Edward Carter, Jones's successor as Surveyor of the King's Works. For most of the conflict, the Compton family were away from Castle Ashby, fighting for the King in the area of their other seat, Compton Wynyates in Warwickshire.

A Compton relative was Bishop of London, and after falling out with the Catholic King James, whom he criticized for too much 'Romanizing' of the Church of England, he retreated for two years to some fine oak-panelled rooms at Castle Ashby. James had seven bishops tried for sedition, and on the day they were acquitted, Henry Compton was one of the signatories to the document asking William of Orange to accept the crown. No doubt to celebrate his part in this great political upheaval, King William III came to dine at Castle Ashby in October 1695, in a room still known as King William's Dining Room.

This room has a very fine, early 17th-century plaster ceiling and some heavy wooden panelling. The chief treasure of the room, though, is its embroidery – thirteen panels, depicting scenes from English rural life, covering two walls from the dado to the ceiling, a height of ten feet or more.

These were worked by the Ladies Penelope and Margaret Compton, and presented to their nephew, the 8th Earl, in 1772. Lady Margaret was sixty-eight when she made her gift, her sister Penelope having died nine years earlier, aged sixty-seven. It was a work of dedication, and a great achievement. But it was not one that oppressed either of the craftswomen for the scenes are neither stiff nor classical representations of a stylized English idyll. Dogs bark at geese; pigs feed busily at a trough; poppies shine out scarlet against a field of corn. The scale of the work is breathtaking, only slightly marred by the knowledge that the colours, so harmoniously muted now, once sang brightly from the walls of this distinguished dining room.

Castle Ashby is not open to the public for tours but is used as a conference centre, and for functions. Parties of embroiderers frequently arrange visits to admire the panels. The house contains other textiles of interest: three Flemish tapestries woven after designs by David Teniers, including a wedding party scene, and several other Mortlake tapestries, bought direct from the factory in about 1632. Early 16th-century tapestry panels in a lobby depict The Fates, woven with gold thread, according to the custom of the Brussels factory at that date. Unfortunately, these were cut up from the whole, reputedly given to the family by Queen Elizabeth after her visit.

The Castle Ashby panels are full of lively realism, but the borders, like this one, have a sophisticated elegance and are suitable for adaptations in needlepoint.

At Castle Ashby, seat of the Earls of Northampton, the dining room is panelled with the work of two ladies of the house, a rich scene of English rural life.

104

*The reaper and his donkey cart, set against the decorative brickwork of the cottage and the bending oak show how cleverly various elements are balanced in the composition of the Castle Ashby panels. This scene makes a naive but stylized picture on its own.*

108

## Rural Scene

| | |
|---|---|
| | 862 |
| □ | 863 |
| | 931 |
| ☑ | 745 |
| | 464 |
| A | 462 |
| | 461 |
| ☑ | 451 |
| ☒ | 433 |
| ◉ | 202 |
| ⊡ | 441 |
| ⊟ | 400 |
| ⊞ | 752 |
| ╱ | 522 |
| ◉ | 520 |
| ◙ | 521 |
| ⊟ | 652 |
| ■ | 650 |
| ■ | 421 |
| ⊡ | 923 |
| | 511 |
| B | 502 |
| | 581 |
| ⊞ | 743 |
| ☒ | 750 |
| | 513 |
| C | 523 |
| | 584 |

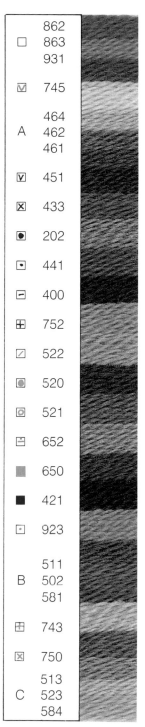

**Calculating Yarn Amounts:**
See page 121.
**Canvas requirements:** To make a picture 47cms/18½ins by 43cms/17ins you will need 62cms/24½ins by 58cms/23ins of 10 holes to the inch mesh. Notice that the background colours are combinations of three subtly different shades – use one strand of each when stitching.

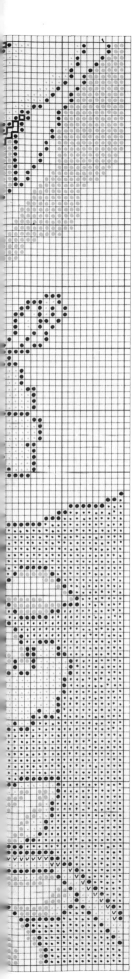

## Primrose

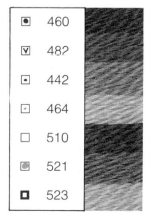

| | |
|---|---|
| ◉ | 460 |
| ☑ | 482 |
| ⊡ | 442 |
| ⊡ | 464 |
| ☐ | 510 |
| ◙ | 521 |
| ◼ | 523 |

**Calculating Yarn Amounts:**
See page 121.
**Canvas requirements:** To
make a 38cm/15in square
cushion you will need
53cms/21ins square of 10
holes to the inch mesh.

*This primrose detail from
the panels at Castle Ashby
reveal the artistry of the
stitchwork. The veins and
shading of the leaves are as
refined as a 17th-century
Dutch flower painting.*

# THE BRONTË SISTERS' SAMPLER AND PURSE

## Haworth Parsonage

No one visiting the home of the Brontë family in Haworth, Yorkshire, can remain unaffected by the remarkable location of this simple parsonage. The view from the rooms at the front of the house is of tombstones and the church beyond; behind, almost immediately available from the back door, is the wilderness of the moors. It is a strange conjunction of images, and one which suits the intensity and intelligent imagination of the Brontë sisters, Charlotte, Emily and Anne.

The children lived in this atmospheric bleak spot for most of their lives. Their mother died in 1821, and her much-loved sister, Aunt Branwell, became their housekeeper, taking care of the girls, their brother Patrick Branwell and Irish-born father, Patrick.

For a brief period, all the daughters were sent to boarding school, but two elder sisters died there in 1825. The school was described for posterity as the dreadful Lowood, in *Jane Eyre*, by Charlotte. After that, the three surviving girls stayed home at Haworth. Aunt Branwell gave them simple lessons and taught them sewing and home management. The numerous samplers still to be seen at the parsonage are dated from this period.

Later in her life, Charlotte became a governess, which she hated, and which is also depicted in *Jane Eyre*. Emily preferred to tend her garden at Haworth, and turned to the moors, to a life of mysticism and solitude. Anne spent much of her time reading religious and philosophical books.

In 1842, Aunt Branwell financed a trip to Brussels for Charlotte and Emily to improve their languages, with a view to opening a small school at Haworth. As is known from the pages of Charlotte's novel, *Villette*, she fell in love with the master of the school, Constantin Héger. She describes herself as dowdy and shy in the novel's heroine Lucy Snowe, but her unique spirit is unmistakable too. The little Florentine pattern purse shown here was made by Charlotte while in Brussels; it is most delicate in colouring and the stitchery is of a particularly fine precision and quality.

Nothing came of the school at Haworth. No parents replied to the published prospectus, and when Branwell returned home after a failed love affair and sank himself in drink, the chance of running such an institution became remote indeed.

An alternative means of income had to be found: the sisters wrote a small volume of verse under the names of Currer, Ellis and Acton Bell. It was published in 1846. Charlotte was then thirty and after her next work, *The Professor*, based on her experience in Brussels, was rejected she turned to the then popular form, the three-volume novel, and produced *Jane Eyre*. On its publication it became a best-seller, and was shortly followed by Emily's masterpiece, *Wuthering Heights*, and Anne's *Agnes Grey*, published together. The sisters had found not only their means of survival but fame. They continued to live at Haworth until Emily's death, in 1848, and Anne's death in 1849. Charlotte left it only for trips to friends, or to London as part of her literary life. She married in 1854, and lived happily at the parsonage with her husband, until her death less than a year later.

The three Brontë sisters, from the left, Anne, Emily and Charlotte were painted by their brother Branwell. This is one of the few authenticated portraits.

This pretty sampler by Emily Brontë provides border ideas and an alphabet. All the sisters were skilled at needlework, one of many interests they shared.

ABCDEFG HIJKLMNOPQ
RSTVUWXYZ 1224567 8
910111213141516171819 &

abcdefghijklmno pqrstvu
wxyz& 20212223 2425

Emily Jane Brontë Finished this Sampler
April the 22nd 1828.

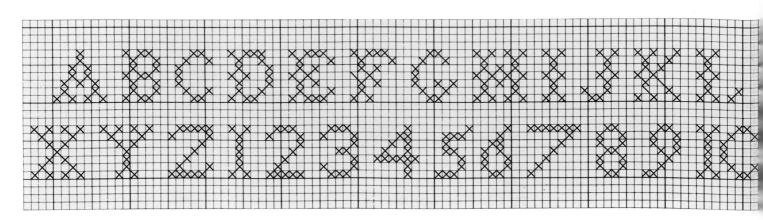

*This beautiful little purse was made by Charlotte Brontë, probably at the time of her stay in Brussels, at the school which later featured in the novel* Villette. *It is finely worked in a combination of flame, tent and cross stitch.*

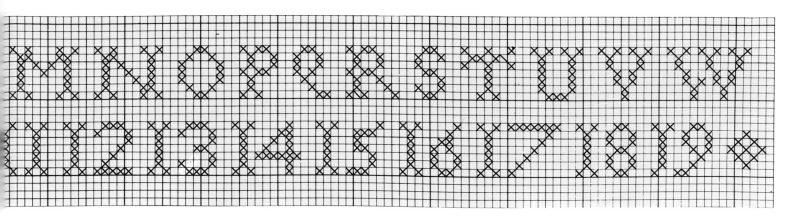

centre

### Haworth Purse

| A | 564 |
|---|-----|
| B | 562 |
| C | 512 |
| D | 510 |
| ■ | 431 |
| ⊙ | 485 |
| ☑ | 491 |
| ☐ | 561 |
| ⊡ | 203 |

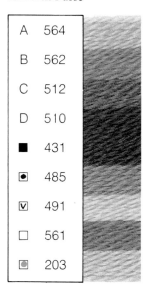

**Calculating Yarn Amounts:** See page 121.
**Canvas requirements:** To make this purse you will need 41cms/16ins by 36cms/14ins of 12 holes to the inch mesh.

# TULIP SEAT COVER
## Arniston

The estate of Arniston House in Midlothian was originally known by the evocative name of Ballintrodo and was granted by King David to the Knights Templars in the 12th century. In 1571, George Dundas bought the land for his eldest son, and it became known then as Arniston. George's grandson, Robert, the 2nd Lord Arniston, laid the foundations for great improvements which were carried out by his own son in turn.

In the 18th century, Robert Dundas, was 1st President of the Court of Session, the Supreme Court of Scotland, a loyal Whig, and a Member of Parliament. His political career was shortlived, however, for after three years he argued with his Government about the introduction of a malt tax which was grossly unfair to the Scots, and was dismissed from office as a result. He retired to his estate and turned his attention to his domestic affairs, commissioning William Adam, one of the leaders of the neo-classical revival, to design a new building and a landscape setting for it.

Most of the house was built between 1726 and 1732, at which point Robert Dundas ran out of funds. His son, Robert Dundas, the 2nd President, also Lord Advocate and MP for Midlothian, continued with the improvements. Drawings for the house by John Adam and dated 1755 are kept at Arniston. The plan was altered a little from his father's concept, for the original three storeys were reduced to two, and the principal drawing room and dining room were formed on the first floor not the floor above. Some of the more formal elements of the garden scheme were altered too, a 'Wilderness' and a parterre demolished, making the house more in keeping with the later 18th-century taste for romantic, apparently natural landscape.

Only brief notes survive on the domestic side of Arniston's history, although the Dundas family have been loyal supporters of Scotland's cause, great lawyers, and responsible farmers for centuries. We do know that the Dundas family were established in the land by the late 1100s, and that Katharine Oliphant, second wife of George Dundas, was a fine needlewoman who 'provided the estate of Arniston for her son out of the proceeds of her pin money'. One of her pieces, intended as a table covering, hangs on a wall at Arniston, and was completed in 1595. It is worked in an unusual stitch, resembling chain stitch in appearance, but is actually two horizontal stitches that produce a V-shape on the right side. The background stitchery is worked in stripes, to give the appearance of a woven tapestry.

Arniston is a beautiful house, with its wonderful double steps to the south porch recently restored. In the main part, the house has by default reverted to the plan originally made in the 1730s – a dry rot outbreak in the 1960s gutted most of the John Adam additions, including the dining and drawing rooms. The present owners, Mr and Mrs A.R. Dundas-Bekker, are refurbishing the house as time and money allow and are devoted to Arniston's survival.

The house is not generally open to the public, but visits can be arranged by letter. It is not known who embroidered the pretty chair with the tulip patterned seat, or when it came to the house, but it needs little recommendation other than its simplicity and finely-balanced colouring.

This little figure is taken from a table covering made by Katharine Oliphant, wife to one of the Dundas family, Lords of Arniston. She was a renowned needlewoman.

The beautiful chair seat cover at Arniston is embroidered in brick stitch, which is very quick to work and a medieval forerunner of Florentine stitch.

**Arniston Tulips**

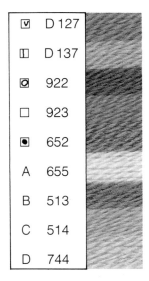

| | |
|---|---|
| ☑ | D 127 |
| ⊞ | D 137 |
| ◙ | 922 |
| ☐ | 923 |
| ◉ | 652 |
| A | 655 |
| B | 513 |
| C | 514 |
| D | 744 |

**Calculating Yarn Amounts:**
See page 121.
**Canvas requirements:** To
make the bag featured
opposite you will need
58cms/23ins by 53cms/21ins
of '0 holes to the inch mesh.

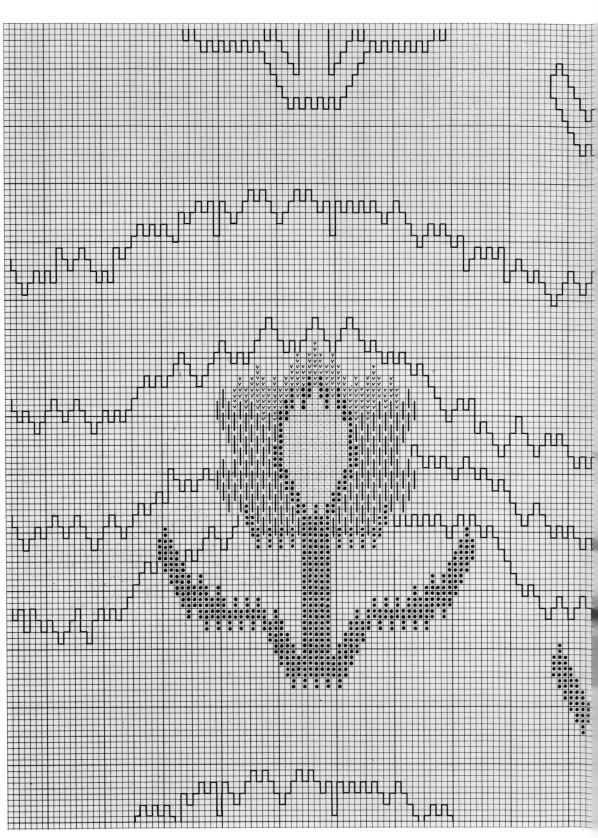

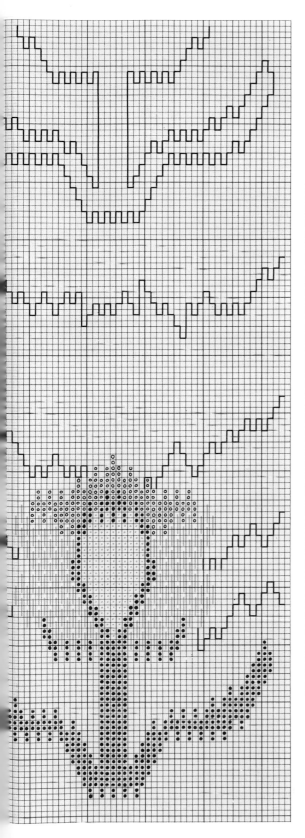

*The brick stitch of the tulip chain was adapted to be worked over four not two holes, for this bag. A bold colouring suggests an alternative effect to the original pastels.*

# EQUIPMENT

## YARNS AND THREADS

All the designs in this book have numbers referring to the colours of Paterna Persian yarn. This is widely available in both the UK and the USA, where it originated in 1916 due to the experimental efforts of two oriental rug and tapestry experts, Harry and Karnig Paternayan (another name by which the yarn is often known). The entire range has more recently arrived in the UK and is available at leading specialist shops throughout the country.

The reason for its superiority over other threads is that the yarn is polished during its manufacture, producing a lovely sheen. The colour range is brilliant and extensive. Also, only the first, long wool shearings are used in the spinning, giving a thread which is much less hairy since the individual strands are longer and finer. Paterna Persian is consequently more durable because there is less abrasion of the hairs as it is worked.

On page 128 a list of alternative colour numbers are given for DMC tapestry yarn colours. Colbert DMC are long-standing reliable products, available internationally on a very wide distribution.

There are numerous other threads that can be used for needlepoint work, some purpose-made and others more commonly used for free-hand embroidery. They may appeal to you more, or work very well for details or special effects.

Thread names are confusing since the word 'tapestry' is often applied to the craft of needlepoint although in truth it refers to woven textile work. It is used mistakenly because the overall effect of fine needlepoint can look similar to tapestry. 'Canvaswork' is an alternative word used in the UK, perhaps more than America. To make matters worse, one of the most common yarns used for needlepoint is known generically as 'tapestry wool' – see below for a description of it. Listed here are the various yarns available, starting with the finest quality, followed by the main types of canvas to match.

**Crewel wool** is a fine, 2-ply, twisted wool thread, used both for crewel embroidery (free embroidery, i.e. not counted thread, usually wool on linen) and for fine grades of needlepoint. Although it is thin, it is very durable and can be used either singly for very minute or outline stitching, or

*The basic essentials: a frame to keep the canvas taut, needles for different canvas mesh, and (l. to r.) 4-ply tapestry, and 2-ply crewel and Persian wool.*

doubled up, so that four plys work each stitch. Always separate out the strands before threading the needle. DMC Medicis has a good range of colours, both bright and soft. Appleton's make another reputable range, with lovely muted colours, available in both the UK and the USA and sold in small quantities. Three strands of Appleton's crewel is equivalent to two of Paterna Persian.

**Persian wool** is a leading brand for needlepoint work and has been described above. It is three strands of 2-ply yarn loosely twisted together, and is useful because the strands can be divided for fine work, or doubled or tripled for coarser needlepoint. It also enables you to mix single threads of different colours to make subtle effects – particularly useful for background work or for plain, tent-stitch embroidery where you might want to add subtlety to the smoothness. If you do mix or add strands of any thread, separate them out first before combining, and do not bother to twist them up together before threading them through the needle. This will avoid tangles and make working smoother.

**Tapestry wool** is a soft feel, 4-ply wool which does not split as readily as crewel or Persian. It is handiest for simple tent-stitch work, e.g. background filling, on

medium canvas, such as 10 mesh mono or double (see later section for canvas types). Tapestry wool is suitable for using double to make rugs on coarser canvases.

With all wool yarns, establish the 'nap' by running the thread across your lips: one way will be rougher, like pushing against fish scales. Be sure to thread the needle so that the nap runs in the direction of work; when the thread is pulled through the canvas it will not be weakened and roughed up. If you use high contrast colours, the darker hairs will catch in the paler.

**Rug wool** has a rougher feel, made in anything from 3- to 8-ply, and designed only for use on coarser canvases, from 5 to 3 mesh. It is best to match the weight of wool to the canvas recommended by the yarn manufacturer because of the variety of plys and thicknesses of wool sold. The type of stitch you use, and the purpose of the rug will also affect the thickness of the yarn you need; for example, Paterna Persian could be used for an ornamental rug, with 6 to 9 strands on a 5 to 4 mesh rug canvas. For working in a cross stitch, half the number of strands would be required as the needle goes through each hole twice (see full chart next page).

Try the effect of reducing the strands by one, where applicable, when working a diagonal stitch, e.g. continental tent stitch; this can produce an equally good effect and will save on the yarn.

Most of the designs in this book are intended for stitching in crewel, Persian or tapestry wool, but that does not preclude experimenting. For example, the background of the Blair Castle flower vase picture (page 91) could be beautiful if worked in reverse tent stitch or another texture stitch, in a shiny cotton perle thread, or even with some painterly sweeps of metallic thread. The same applies to the Wallington strawberry or swan (pages 29 and 30) which could look extremely fine worked on a smaller mesh of canvas in soft embroidery cottons. These 'embroidery flosses', as they are also known, are made in a vast range of colours. As they come in six strands, however, they are a little tricky to use with the thread doubled through the needle (it takes time to pull the twelve strands evenly flat). Since they are not nearly as durable as fine wool they are only recommended for purely decorative work.

## TAPESTRY NEEDLES

The correct needle to use has a long, slim eye, and a blunt end. This is essential. Sharp points can split the canvas unnecessarily, and you cannot unpick work if a sharp needle has run through previous stitches. A sharp point will also reduce your fingertips to a pincushion, particularly if you are working at a frame. A time-saving system is to thread all the different colours you require at one time in separate needles, and have them pinned nearby, ready for use. As you stitch, move the needle up the thread occasionally to avoid wear at one spot, and a thin patch. The optimum length of yarn to thread is about 46cms/18ins. A useful device is a piece of card cut to half that length. Wind the thread needed around it and cut through all the yarn at one end to make a hank of lengths, ready when required.

You may find it helpful to use a needle slightly larger than the canvas hole size so that it stretches the hole slightly as you stitch. When the embroidery is eventually blocked, the holes revert to shape and give a tight finish.

## CANVASES

There are three types of canvas and they are still only made to imperial measurements: mono (or single thread), double (or Penelope), and interlock. Others exist, ranging from plastic, or PVC, and polyester canvas, to very fine silk gauzes. Polyester canvas is useful for embroideries that will be used on clothing. Most popular canvases are made of cotton, but high-quality linen or hemp is sometimes found in the finer meshes. Normally there is a choice of two colours of cotton canvas, white and ecru. White suits pale work, and the ecru is usually hidden by darker stitching. Alternatively, the canvas can be painted with colourfast dyes or pencils before use, and sometimes pretty effects can be made by painting canvas, leaving areas visible around the embroidery. The Blair Castle flower vase picture (page 91) could be given this treatment.

**Mono (or single thread) canvas** is woven with single threads in each direction, and commonly used by beginners who find the double threads confusing. It is stiffer than double canvas which helps to keep

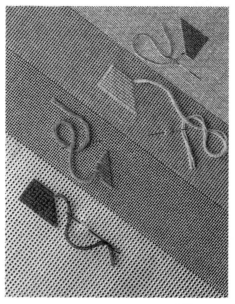

*There is a wide range of canvases available. Here are four of the most frequently used ones: plastic (7 mesh), mono (10 and 16 mesh) and double (12 mesh).*

stitches regular for the less experienced and if not using a frame. Others find this lack of pliability less pleasant to the touch. Mono is the type most often found in ready-made kits. It is available in sizes from 32 to 10 holes per inch.

**Double (or Penelope) canvas** has two threads running in each direction. This is useful if the embroidery is to be 'trammed', that is, when threads of the same colour as the stitch to be worked over the top are run flat across the double threads to add bulk and strength to the work. The stitchery is then worked over the base thread. Tramming may be time-consuming but it does save referring to a chart all the time, and some people like to do it for this reason – particularly for geometric work, like flame stitch patterns.

A second main purpose of double canvas is that you can push the double threads apart to be evenly spaced and work this area in stitches half the size of the surround – *petit point*. This could be used to good effect, for example, on the Burghley cherub picture (page 60) where the leaves could be worked in a large tent stitch and the flesh tones in finer needlepoint, perhaps in a silkier thread.

Double canvas is essential if you prefer to work tent stitch by the half-cross stitch method otherwise the stitch is not

anchored between the holes. Double is usually more pliable than mono canvas, but which works best is a matter of experiment and personal preference. It is available in sizes from 12 to 8 holes per inch.

**Interlock canvas,** as its name suggests, has double vertical threads bonded or twisted round two horizontal threads. It looks and works as a mono canvas, however. It is manufactured in a variety of sizes from 18 to 5 holes per inch. Interlock is useful for rug making because it is particularly stable. It is handy, too, for very small objects where the edges are to be overcast with a special stitch or bound with tape or other material. The rug canvas sizes are often made with a brown stripe marking regular squares, useful for planning designs and counting stitches.

**Plastic canvas** is a new development worth noting because it is ideal for small projects, such as napkin rings or Christmas tree decorations. It can be cut and trimmed in one, so it is ideal for making little jewel or 'house' boxes, decorative table mats, and so on. It is very stiff and only available in coarse hole sizes. Small squares and circles are sold ready-cut too.

Canvases are sold in different widths, ranging from 48 to 152cms/19 to 60ins. Balance out whether you should buy just enough in a small width for the single project in hand, or whether buying more and putting the remainder aside for other work later, would be more economical. A metre/yard of a wider canvas might give you material for four cushions whereas a metre/yard of a narrower one might only give you two, with some wastage. Kits work similarly. They are economical if you wish to work just that one object but they can work out to be more expensive than buying all the ingredients separately or using materials that you have to hand.

## CALCULATING YARN AMOUNTS

It is impractical to give yarn amounts for the charts in this book because the 'take-up' of yarn varies considerably with the stitch and canvas employed. First, mono canvas is more economic of yarn than double. Second, many of the designs in this book are intended to be worked in

121

tent stitch and there are four different ways of working this stitch alone, some using less yarn than others. The choice of tent-stitch method depends on use; for example, the vertical method is economic, but not hard-wearing: since your technique will vary with each project, the amount of yarn used will vary too.

The following is a general guide to the amount of yarn needed for the four canvases used in this book: working on 5 mesh canvas and working in cross stitch, 70cms/28ins of 3 strands of Persian wool will cover 1in square. On 10 mesh mono canvas, using Continental tent stitch, 10cms/43ins of yarn will cover 1in square. On 14 mesh, 154cms/61ins of yarn and on 22 mesh, 262cms/104ins of yarn will cover 1in square.

The formula for calculating yarn quantities is to work a small square, say 2.5cms/1in, in the canvas, in stitch type and yarn you wish to use. Measure the yarn length taken up, and multiply this by the total area of the design. Now roughly measure the areas of each colour. Add up individual colour amounts, and if it comes close to the total coverage figure, you have an accurate guide as to amounts.

This is not as onerous as it sounds. You can tell at a glance if you need less than a metre/yard for little patches of colour. Larger areas are easy to measure anyway, just by eye, rather than counting little squares. Experience soon makes calculating easy to do – but the key step is finding out the stitch technique you prefer to use, particularly for tent stitch, and how much yarn it takes up on the canvas of your choice. When buying colours always buy colours of the same dye-lot, usually marked on the paper label: buy a generous amount to avoid matching problems at a later date.

| CANVAS mono mesh | PERSIAN STRANDS vertical or horizontal stitch | DMC STRANDS vertical or horizontal stitch | NEEDLE SIZES |
|---|---|---|---|
| 22, 24 | 1 | MEDICIS 1 | 24 |
| 20 | 1 | 1 | 22 |
| 18 | 1 | 2 | 19, 20 |
| 16 | 2 | 2 | 19, 20 |
| 14 | 3 | TAPESTRY 1 | 18, 20 |
| 12 | 3 | 1 | 17, 18 |
| 10 | 3 | 1 | 17, 18 |
| 7 | 4 | 2 | 15, 16 |
| 4, 5 | 6-9 | 2 | 15, 16 |

# STITCHES

**Continental tent stitch** is worked with the needle held diagonally, but in horizontal or vertical rows producing a thick ridge of yarn at the back of the mesh. It is hard-wearing, and tends not to distort the canvas. It is the most suitable stitch for chair seats, rugs, buckled belts, etc. Of course, as it effectively wraps round two threads, it eats up the yarn, using double the amount of half-cross stitch.

**Basket-weave tent stitch** produces a woven effect on the back of the canvas. It is quick to work and recommended for filling in large background areas of colour. Like the continental stitch, you work one stitch to the right and under two threads of canvas, but cover the canvas diagonally. Work from the top left-hand corner of the canvas downwards in little blocks.

**Half-cross tent stitch** is recognizable on the reverse because it only covers the holes of the canvas, and leaves one direction of the threads visible between the stitches. It looks like lines of backstitch and can be worked horizontally or vertically. Economic of thread, it is best used for purely decorative tent-stitch projects, like pictures, frames, napkin rings, brooches and so on (such as those featured on pages 45 and 63).

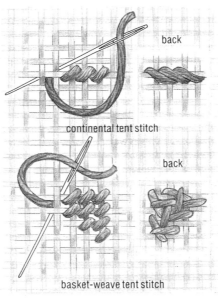

back

continental tent stitch

back

basket-weave tent stitch

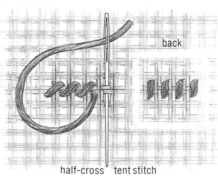

back

half-cross tent stitch

On practising these stitches, most people will find that they remember a method from childhood or school that seems lodged in the fingers, and easier to work. There are no rules; in fact many people use a combination of tent-stitch methods without feeling too ashamed of themselves. It is best to work to a level of technique that suits you at the time – progress is sure that way, and you can get on to refining in your own good time.

This is by no means a comprehensive survey of other needlepoint stitches, but here are a few alternatives that relate particularly well to the designs in this book, with suggestions for their use.

**Straight stitches. Counted satin stitch** is one of the basic straight stitches that are easy to do, cover space quickly, and are easily varied. It is useful for background filling and could be used for the sky or water areas of a number of the charts in this book, e.g. the Wallington swan picture (page 30), or the Burghley House flowers, if used individually (pages 64-5).

**Parisian stitch** is another straight stitch, which makes a pretty background alternative. It could be used successfully on the roof area of the little house picture in Castle Ashby (page 106).

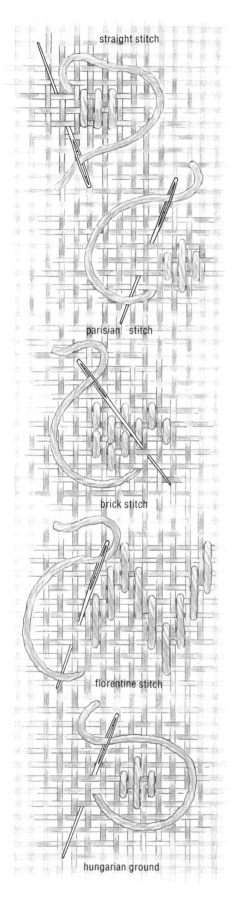

straight stitch

parisian stitch

brick stitch

florentine stitch

hungarian ground

**Brick stitch,** the forerunner of Bargello or Florentine work, is worked in a regular step arrangement, and stitched in straight lines in every other hole in the row – the stitches of the second row fill in the gap.

**Florentine stitch** is also worked in a step arrangement, but the length of the stitches can be endlessly varied, e.g. 4 step then 2 step, repeated alternately. Several charts in this book show variations on these stitches.

**Hungarian ground and Hungarian point** produce diamond shapes as the rows grow. Hungarian stitch varies the units over only three rows of canvas; Hungarian point uses a row of long stitches over six or seven threads, followed by several rows of stitches over a smaller number of threads making a subsidiary zigzag effect.

**Diagonal stitches. Cross stitch** is used for the Wallington nursery rug (page 26), on a fine scale for the Haworth sampler (page 113), and could also be used in a number of other projects – for example in a silk or cotton thread on linen for the Burghley House cherub picture (page 62). It is durable and easy to make regular because of its symmetrical, self-correcting shape, one diagonal crossed by another. It can be worked in long lines to the left, and reversing to the right over the first row.

**Upright cross stitch** is a useful background stitch which could be used in conjunction with the orthodox stitch, say for the Wallington sampler (pages 24-5).

**Rice stitch** produces a richly textured effect, too, with an extra small cross made on the spokes of a larger one. It could be introduced into the working of the Castle Ashby country picture (page 106).

**Mosaic stitch** is an attractive alternative diagonal stitch, forming little boxes. Use it as a background filling stitch, for example, on the Leeds Castle belt (page 44) or the Belton House orange tree tieback (page 76).

**Cashmere stitch** is a little similar and produces a rich, tapestry effect; useful perhaps as background filling for the Glamis Castle motifs as pictures or cushion covers (pages 11 and 12).

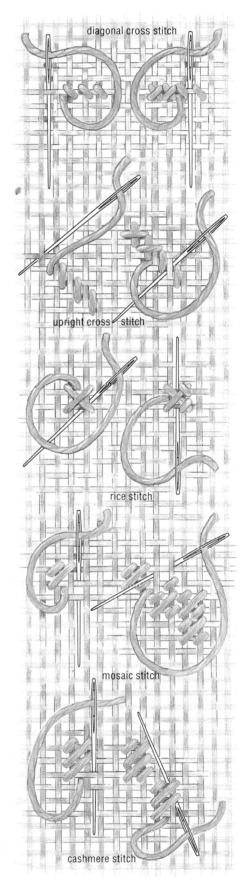

diagonal cross stitch

upright cross stitch

rice stitch

mosaic stitch

cashmere stitch

123

# STARTING AND FINISHING OFF

To begin, always use a piece of canvas several cms/ins larger than the area to be covered by stitchery. Double-fold the edges in and tack around, or cover raw edges with adhesive sticky tape – otherwise your thread will catch on the rough canvas edges all the time, which is exasperating. If necessary, run a line of coloured thread through the centre of the canvas, top to bottom and horizontally, to help you centre the design and count out the squares from the graph charts. Run tacking guidelines elsewhere, too, should you need them.

A good way to begin needlepoint is to tie a knot, pass the thread through from the front to the back of the canvas a little distance from the start of your row, and work your stitches along the row covering the thread. Cut off the knot once you have secured the thread.

To finish a thread, a similar method applies: leave the end-thread hanging loose until you come back to it on the second row of your new thread. Hold it under a few of the stitches on this row, to secure, then cut the spare end off. Do not prise up stitches on the back of the canvas and run the finishing end underneath them as this spoils the tension and even appearance of the stitches on the front of the canvas.

## BLOCKING AND SETTING

Cover a piece of chipboard, blockboard, cork or other similar, inexpensive soft wood substance with a sheet of paper; either dressmakers' graph paper or plain paper. It should have the finished shape of your needlepoint piece drawn on it – in a colourfast waterproof marker.

Some brave people wash their finished work, immersing it in a good-quality wool washing agent, and block it when damp. (DMC do not recommend this practice.) Others prefer just to spray the back of the piece liberally with water to make it stretchy and pliable for blocking. If your work is grubby and you have any doubt about the yarn used, have the piece drycleaned before blocking it, and merely damp it with a fine water spray.

Lay the work face down and pull it gently into the required shape. You may have to damp and dry several times before the work conforms naturally to the exact outline. Pin out the canvas working on alternate sides – i.e. one pin on the left, one on the right, one top, one bottom, and so on. Leave to dry for at least a day.

## FRAMES

One of the advantages of canvaswork is that it is readily portable. Working on a frame obviously cancels out that feature. All the designs in this book can be successfully completed without using a frame. There is no doubt, however, that frames ensure work is taut, evenly stitched, and kept in shape. Newer table-top models are useful for disabled embroiderers, with an adjustable stand so that only one hand is needed for working. Floor-mounted models are useful for big projects.

A roller frame has two rollers top and bottom, to which strips of canvas are attached. The canvas is lined up square and oversewn firmly to these border strips. The area of canvas not being worked is then rolled out of the way. The rollers screw tight into vertical laths at each side, thus completing the frame. The sides of the canvas are kept taut by lacing them to the vertical laths with a chenille needle and string or other strong thread. Most frames are not more than 30cms/12ins in depth, so large pieces of work involve quite a lot of winding on and relacing.

Slate frames have screw grooves all down the side laths, so that the depth of the frame can be varied easily and the work kept very taut. Floor-standing frames may cause you to bend forward constantly over your embroidery, so try to sit at one and ensure that they suit you physically before buying one.

## SMALL ACCESSORIES

Try not to use pencil for marking up a canvas; graphite makes yarns very grubby. Alternatively, embroidery stores sell marker pens and special acrylic paints that are recommended for painting or delineating a design before you begin stitching.

A simple accessory you can make for yourself is a 'palette' in stiff card with holes for every colour to be used. The code numbers, names and, most valuably, chart symbols, can be written at the side of each one. Loop the cut lengths of yarn through the appropriate hole.

# MAKING UP

## CUSHIONS

Several of the charts in this book are designed for making into cushions – probably the most common and versatile of canvaswork projects.

**Appliquéd cushions** The quickest way to display your finished needlepoint is merely to trim and turn under the raw edges and appliqué the finished shape to the front of a slightly larger, ready-made cushion cover. This is an ideal method to feature small circular motifs such as the Burghley House flowers (pages 64-5). If you choose a handsome velvet or similar quality fabric, and if you were to take the trouble to use a decorative border stitch to attach the canvas, say a cross or herringbone stitch, worked in two colours, this could look very attractive. Alternatively, use a ribbon trim to cover the canvas edge.

**Simple stitched cushions** Another method is to make a cushion using the entire piece of needlepoint for the front and a good-quality furnishing textile for the back. If a needlepoint design has a border effect in its stitchery, like the Chastleton rose (page 103), then there is no need to create a border for the front. However, if you prefer to attach a border, e.g. for the Glamis Castle motifs (pages 11 and 12), choose a fabric of the same weight as the canvaswork. Velvet, heavy slub silk (or dupion), or firm linen can look attractive, though in general, needlepoint looks best speaking for itself without fabric added to it. Simply place the finished needlepoint right sides together with the backing fabric, stitch all round three sides and a little round the corners of the fourth side. Turn the cover right side out, insert a cushion pad, and slipstitch the join.

Note that these cushions will always need to be drycleaned, to preserve the needlepoint, and because the different fabrics may shrink at different rates, and ruin your work.

## Materials
(for an average 38cms/15ins square or round cushion):
**backing fabric:** 75cms/¾yd
**zip:** 25cms/10ins

1. Cut a section for the cushion back allowing 1.5cms/¾in on all sides for seams and allowing 3.5cms/1½ins in the centre of the piece for inserting a zip. (For a circle, take a 3.5cm/1½in pleat in the centre of the fabric before cutting out.) Cut the back fabric in half at the centre, join two small seams at each side of this gap, leaving space in the middle for the zip. Tack the zip into position. Stitch the zip into the centre back.

2. Trim the edge of the embroidered canvas front leaving 2.5cms/1in seam allowances. Open the zip in the back section. Place the canvas on the backing fabric, right sides together. Tack and stitch front and back together. Trim away excess seam allowance, snipping at corners. Turn to right side and insert cushion pad.

## PICTURES AND FRAMES
Hand-made picture frames are inexpensive to make, and an original way to display your needlepoint skill. A similar method will make a mirror frame too. For very fine work, a card frame may have to be covered in cheap plain cotton as a lining, using exactly the same method as for the needlepoint itself.

### Materials
**stiff card:** two pieces cut to the dimension of the surround
**fabric glue**
**twisted cord trim:** length to fit circumference of frame
**soft felt, fabric or hessian:** small piece for backing frame
**craft blade knife,** e.g. Stanley knife
**metal rule, drawing pins**

1. Cut the stiff card to the outside measurement using a sharp blade knife and a metal ruler (wood or plastic rulers can be ruined, sliver-cut by the blade).

2. Cut out the inside frame for the picture. This will eventually be covered by fabric, so do not worry about bevelling edges.

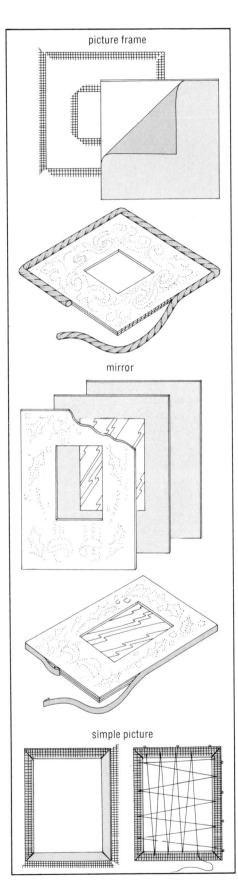

picture frame

mirror

simple picture

3. Trim the needlepoint canvas piece leaving 5cms/2ins spare canvas on inside and outside edges. If desired, cut a piece of lining fabric to the same shape and mount it to the card first, as described in Step 5.

4. Use drawing pins to position needlepoint accurately over front side of cardboard, matching edges neatly. Cut away excess canvas at corners to avoid bulky turnings.

5. Using fabric glue, gently ease and stick the lining and/or canvas overlap areas to the wrong side of the frame, taking care to keep canvas lines straight on all edges of the frame. If using lining, wait until the glue is dry before mounting the canvas.

6. Cover a single backing piece of card on one side only with felt (this does not fray so there is no need to overlap the edges), or other suitable fabric (in which case turn edges to wrong side of card and glue).

7. When both cards are dry, place picture between frame and back, and overstitch neatly round the frame and back edges to join. Trim by slipstitching or whip stitching a handsome cord over the joined edges, making final join at bottom centre.

**For a mirror:** use a very stiff card, the same thickness as a small hand, or cosmetic, mirror or cheap mirror tile, and cut one frame section, so that the mirror fits exactly in the hole. Now cut a second frame section with a slightly smaller 'window' to be the actual frame. Cut a third piece the same size to be the back.

Cover the frame section and the backing piece as described above. Stitch all these layers together. In place of corded trim, use a velvet or other ribbon to cover the thicker raw edges, folding and joining ends at bottom centre.

Larger mirrors should be treated as framed pictures for safety. The needlepoint will act as the mount, covered as described above. The mirror should be either professionally framed or fitted in a frame kit with a sturdy back. Obviously no glass is needed.

## A SIMPLE PICTURE
A simple way to present needlepoint as a picture is to cut a piece of thin wood or stiff

card to the exact dimensions of the finished embroidery. (Cardboard contains acid which will rot fibres with time. Do not use it for work you hope to keep a long time. Plywood is safer.) Cover the board with lining fabric, glueing it to the back. Leave till dry.

Place the embroidery on the covered side, and pull the edges to the wrong side lining up all sides parallel. Use brass pins or tacks to hold and correct the position. The needlepoint can be glued to the back as before (trimming excess out of folded corners) or laced across with strong thread. Lace top and bottom, then side to side. Weave the second direction thread through the first, for a stronger hold.

## LARGE BAG

Choose a stiff, tough fabric: linen, hessian, tapestry-type textile, corduroy, denim. Measure your finished embroidery area. Buy sufficient fabric to be four times this area, allowing for seams. Also calculate fabric required for gussets, the width preferred at the two sides, and base. Buy a small piece of stiff buckram for the base, and contrast bias trim, ready-made, 3-4cms/1½ins wide, or allow extra fabric to cut matching bias yourself.

1. Cut a rectangle: the length should be the depth of the embroidery times four, plus twice the base gusset width. Add seam allowances at either end. Its width should be slightly more than the width of the embroidery: plus seam allowances. Machine stitch to join the narrow edges of the rectangle. Fold so that the seam will sit inside the gusset area of the base. Press the two folds in the long doubled layer of fabric.

2. Cut two lengths for straps. Fold in half, right sides facing, stitch and turn right side out, with the seam flattened to centre back of each one. Topstitch along the edges of the straps if desired.

3. Pin the straps near both folds, which will be the top edges of the bag, front and back. Fasten by stitching in a square and cross for strength.

4. Check position of the embroidery on the front panel of this doubled strip. Pin the embroidery right side facing, with the

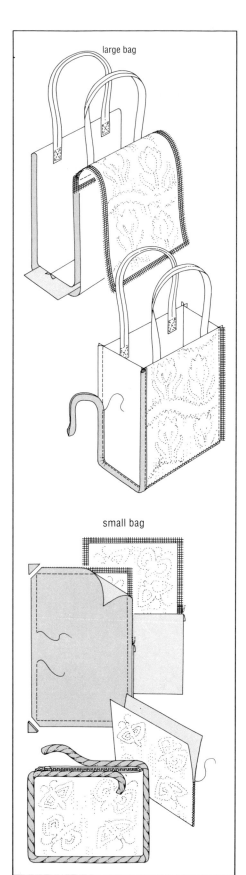

large bag

small bag

seam allowance of the top edge of the embroidery on the top fold of the bag. Stitch, then fold down the embroidery right side out on the front of the bag. Fold in the bottom raw edge of the embroidery and slip stitch to the bottom of the bag front section. Trim canvas edges level with the edges of the fabric if necessary.

5. Cut the buckram to the exact size of the base area, slip between the two layers of fabric and stitch down both long sides to hold in place.

6. Cut double-length gusset pieces for the two sides, fold to align with the folded top edges of the bag. Pin and tack in place, wrong sides together, then machine stitch with the raw edges facing outwards.

7. For strength, machine stitch a bias trim all round these raw edges.

## SMALL BAG

**Materials**
**velvet or other suitable material:** piece same size as bag front
**lining:** piece double length of bag, same width
**zip:** matching and to fit width of bag
**silk twist cord trim:** length to measure circumference of bag plus one width extra

1. Cut the velvet back piece to the dimensions of the embroidered front piece, plus seam allowances. Trim the edges of the needlepoint canvas to leave seam allowances only, and place the two fabric pieces together, right sides facing. Stitch along the bottom edge to join.

2. Cut lining fabric in rectangle to same size as bag (front and back joined) plus seam allowances on all edges.

3. Right sides together, stitch all round lining and joined canvas and velvet, leaving a small gap at one long side. Trim corners and turn through to right side.

4. Fold in half, right side outside, and overstitch side seams to join.

5. Stitch cord trim on all edges: start at one corner of top opening, along top back edge, down side, along bottom seam, along second side seam, and then along

remaining top edge. Push the two ends of cord into each top corner of the bag and secure. Sew zip along top opening.

## JEWELRY ROLL

**Materials**

**lining fabric:** scraps to fit canvaswork
**ribbon or more lining fabric:** scraps to make loops or pockets
**bias binding:** in contrast colour
**interfacing:** small piece to fit canvaswork

1. Cut a rectangle of lining material, and a rectangle of soft interfacing, such as flannel or muslin. Trim seam allowances from the interlining and lightly slipstitch to the wrong side of the canvaswork.

2. Fold small scraps of lining material to make small straps, or use matching velvet ribbon, and stitch in a series of loops to the lining material to hold necklaces.

3. Alternatively, make a series of little pockets: cut two narrow strips of lining, same size as the lining rectangle. Fold in half, and press short ends in to neaten. Stitch the strips to the lining piece, with the folded edges facing to the centre of the lining rectangle, and stitching divisions along the strips to make small pockets.

4. Stitch this lining to the canvaswork, wrong sides together. One short end of the canvaswork can be trimmed to a point if desired. Enclose all raw edges together with bias binding in a colour which matches the lining.

5. Take a length of matching velvet or satin ribbon, fold in half, and stitch the centre to the pointed end of the roll. Wrap round the roll to tie.

## SIMPLE BELT OR TIE-BACK

To make a belt or tie-back more substantial, cut a piece of iron-on interfacing (available in a number of different thicknesses) to the exact shape of the finished belt or tie-back. Following manufacturer's instructions, apply this to the lining material before cutting out, but not right on an edge to allow for turnings.

1. Cut a scrap of lining material to the

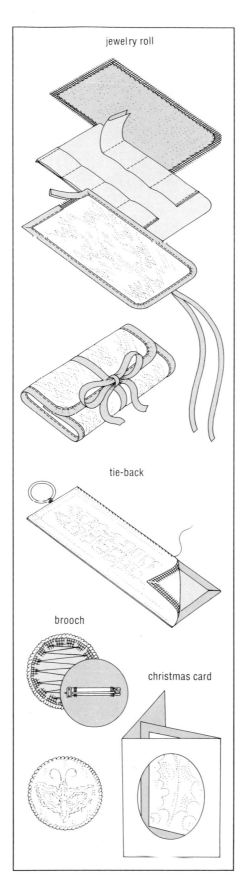

jewelry roll

tie-back

brooch

christmas card

same shape as the needlepoint, with seam allowances on all sides. Fold in the seam allowances and press. (If pre-stiffened, the seam allowance should fold round the iron-on area neatly.)

2. Trim and fold in 1cm/½in all round the belt or tie-back canvas and tack to hold down. Snip into corners and trim away extra bulk in folds.

3. Place lining and canvaswork wrong sides together, and overstitch all round the edges. The stitches sink neatly into the wool.

4. **For a belt:** buy a suitable buckle, preferably without a prong but with some other bar-closing device. Attach according to type.

5. **For tie-backs:** stitch a small brass ring to each end of the tie-back and hold to the wall on a cup hook. Attach decorative ribbons or tassels to each end of the shape if desired.

## BROOCHES

Use 14 mesh mono canvas and complete embroidery. Make an extra row of outline stitches around your motif to allow for mounting. Cut a small disc of stiff card or buckram to the shape of the finished stitchery. Leaving a 1cm/½in allowance all round, cut out the embroidery. Trim triangles of canvas out of the edging. Fold round the card and, using a strong thread, draw in the canvas edges, lacing them at the back over the card taking care not to distort the needlepoint. Cut a small piece of felt to cover the back of the brooch. Slipstitch all round the edges to keep in place and finally stitch a small bar or safety pin to the back.

## CHRISTMAS CARDS

Cut a rectangle three times the required front dimensions of your card, in stiff card. Mark with a pencil three equal sections. Using a craft blade knife, cut a suitable 'window' in the centre panel of card. Now lightly glue the finished piece of needlepoint to the left-hand panel beside it. Fold the card in three, so that the embroidery is enclosed, and the card has a fold at the front left edge.

# ALTERNATIVE YARN NUMBERS

This chart provides you with the corresponding DMC yarn colour codes. Some of the DMC colours have been repeated as the range is not as varied as the Paterna yarns.

For mail order suppliers of DMC yarns write enclosing a stamped and addressed envelope to: Colbert DMC yarns Pullman Road Wigston Leicester LE8 2DY 0533 813919 DMC Corporation 107 Trumbell Street Elizabeth New Jersey 07206 U.S.A. DMC Needlecraft PTY Ltd PO Box 131 Balmore 2192 New South Wales Australia.

| PATERNA | DMC | PATERNA | DMC | PATERNA | DMC | PATERNA | DMC | PATERNA | DMC | PATERNA | DMC |
|---|---|---|---|---|---|---|---|---|---|---|---|
| 200 | 7275 | 442 | 7494 | 531 | 7329 | 644 | 7371 | 743 | 7472 | 906 | 7133 |
| 201 | 7620 | 443 | 7455 | 532 | 7701 | 650 | 7425 | 744 | 7503 | 910 | 7212 |
| 202 | 7321 | 444 | 7579 | 533 | 7337 | 652 | 7363 | 745 | 7905 | 911 | 7210 |
| 203 | 7282 | 450 | 7515 | 541 | 7796 | 655 | 7420 | 750 | 7487 | 912 | 7205 |
| 204 | 7300 | 451 | 7490 | 542 | 7797 | 660 | 7389 | 751 | 7485 | 913 | 7204 |
| 213 | 7715 | 455 | 7461 | 543 | 7798 | 661 | 7387 | 752 | 7474 | 914 | 7151 |
| 220 | NOIR | 460 | 7489 | 545 | 7313 | 662 | 7541 | 753 | 7503 | 920 | 7449 |
| 221 | 7713 | 461 | 7416 | 550 | 7318 | 663 | 7542 | 754 | 7503 | 922 | 7165 |
| 236 | 7280 | 462 | 7415 | 553 | 7313 | 666 | 7400 | 755 | 7579 | 923 | 7193 |
| 246 | 7300 | 463 | 7413 | 561 | 7798 | 670 | 7583 | 756 | 7579 | 924 | 7192 |
| 260 | BLANC | 464 | 7520 | 562 | 7799 | 681 | 7943 | 760 | 7433 | 930 | 7184 |
| 261 | ECRU | 465 | 7450 | 564 | 7715 | 683 | 7911 | 761 | 7434 | 931 | 7184 |
| 262 | ECRU | 470 | 7469 | 571 | 7307 | 686 | 7912 | 763 | 7905 | 932 | 7759 |
| 263 | ECRU | 473 | 7162 | 580 | 7311 | 692 | 7988 | 771 | 7971 | 933 | 7761 |
| 312 | 7895 | 481 | 7169 | 581 | 7650 | 693 | 7548 | 772 | 7435 | 934 | 7761 |
| 321 | 7257 | 482 | 7168 | 582 | 7650 | 696 | 7345 | 773 | 7431 | 940 | 7138 |
| 322 | 7255 | 485 | 7166 | 583 | 7813 | 700 | 7767 | 800 | 7922 | 941 | 7108 |
| 324 | 7251 | 490 | 7164 | 584 | 7813 | 702 | 7742 | 801 | 7919 | 942 | 7640 |
| 330 | 7245 | 491 | 7121 | 585 | 7828 | 703 | 7725 | 803 | 7918 | 943 | 7104 |
| 351 | 7157 | 492 | 7191 | 591 | 7596 | 711 | 7784 | 840 | 7108 | 944 | 7135 |
| 353 | 7153 | 500 | 7536 | 592 | 7596 | 712 | 7726 | 850 | 7303 | 945 | 7133 |
| 400 | 7459 | 501 | 7297 | 595 | 7599 | 714 | 7078 | 851 | 7920 | 948 | 7191 |
| 401 | 7459 | 502 | 7306 | 600 | 7379 | 720 | 7700 | 852 | 7125 | 950 | 7544 |
| 406 | 7162 | 503 | 7802 | 602 | 7426 | 721 | 7445 | 853 | 7922 | 951 | 7849 |
| 410 | 7468 | 504 | 7302 | 603 | 7404 | 722 | 7444 | 861 | 7184 | 952 | 7106 |
| 411 | 7479 | 505 | 7301 | 604 | 7402 | 724 | 7506 | 862 | 1360 | 953 | 7106 |
| 412 | 7845 | 510 | 7288 | 611 | 7320 | 725 | 7742 | 863 | 7214 | 955 | 7103 |
| 413 | 7486 | 511 | 7930 | 612 | 7384 | 726 | 7785 | 871 | 7168 | 961 | 7603 |
| 420 | 7529 | 512 | 7695 | 620 | 7909 | 730 | 7496 | 872 | 7165 | 963 | 7804 |
| 421 | 7533 | 513 | 7293 | 621 | 7911 | 731 | 7833 | 873 | 7214 | 970 | 7666 |
| 422 | 7467 | 514 | 7692 | 623 | 7382 | 732 | 7474 | 874 | 7164 | D127 | 7241 |
| 430 | 7467 | 520 | 7408 | 630 | 7345 | 733 | 7484 | 880 | 7178 | D137 | 7241 |
| 431 | 7499 | 521 | 7327 | 632 | 7344 | 734 | 7473 | 881 | 7446 | D211 | 7198 |
| 433 | 7497 | 522 | 7326 | 633 | 7341 | 735 | 7597 | 901 | 7139 | D389 | 7337 |
| 434 | 7463 | 523 | 7323 | 640 | 7417 | 740 | 7496 | 903 | 7136 | D500 | 7540 |
| 440 | 7497 | 524 | 7599 | 641 | 7425 | 741 | 7485 | 904 | 7135 | D502 | 7956 |
| 441 | 7780 | 530 | 7429 | 642 | 7355 | 742 | 7473 | 905 | 7605 | | |

# USEFUL ADDRESSES

It is possible to visit all of the places featured in this book, but opening times will obviously vary – it is recommended you ring before visiting.

Arniston Gorebridge Lothian 031 225 5124
Belton House Grantham Lincolnshire 0476 66116
Blair Castle Blair Atholl Pitlochry 079681 207/356
Boughton House Geddington Northamptonshire 0536 82248
Burghley House Stamford Lincolnshire 0780 52451
Castle Ashby Northamptonshire 060 129 234
Chastleton near Moreton-in-Marsh Gloucestershire 0608 74 355
Dorney Court Windsor Buckinghamshire 06286 4638
Glamis Castle Glamis Angus 030 784 242
Haworth Parsonage Haworth West Yorkshire 0535 42323
Leeds Castle Maidstone Kent 0622 65400
Standen near East Grinstead West Sussex 0342 230 29
Sudeley Castle Winchcombe Gloucestershire 0242 602308
Uppark near Petersfield West Sussex 073085 317/458
Wallington Cambo Morpeth Northumberland 067 074 283

# LIST OF SUPPLIERS

The Royal School of Needlework 5 King Street Covent Garden London 01 240 7709 (also mail order)
Needle Needs 20 Beauchamp Place London SW3 1NQ 01 589 2361
W H I Tapestry Shop 85 Pimlico Road London SW1W 8PH 01 730 5366

If you have any difficulty in finding Paterna yarns, they will be glad to supply you with a list of suppliers for the UK, USA, Canada or Australia. You can write to them at:
Paterna Yarns NEEDLEART HOUSE M P Stonehouse Ltd P O Box 13 Albion Mills Westgate Wakefield 0924 373456